Russell Ovans is a computer scientist, educator, entrepreneur, father, and frustrated musician. He was the founding CEO of Backstage Technologies, a social game company that pioneered monetization through the sale of virtual currency. Before that he led the development team at AbeBooks.com and was the systems architect at Prophet.Net.

Along the way Dr. Ovans received a Ph.D. in computer science from Simon Fraser University in Vancouver, and taught software engineering at the University of Victoria and Camosun College.

Lord of the Files

Essays on the Social Aspects of Software Engineering

Russell Ovans

Published in Canada by Thought Pilots.

Cover design by Myke Allen.

ISBN-13: 978-0-9869418-0-1

ISBN-10: 0-9869418-0-8

10 9 8 7 6 5 4 3 2 1

Maybe there is a beast… maybe it's only us.
— William Golding, *Lord of the Flies*

The file will henceforth be one of the basic underlying elements
of the human story, like genes.
— Jaron Lanier, *You Are Not a Gadget*

Preface

Software engineering is a social activity; forget that and your career is lost.

Not everyone can be a software engineer. It requires significant proficiency in mathematical reasoning, systems thinking, perseverance, and intelligence to build information storage and retrieval systems using today's abstract programming techniques.

Thus, the goal of computer science curricula is to endow students with the requisite mathematical maturity and problem-solving skills to become good software engineers. However, nothing is typically done to instill students with the requisite plain old maturity needed to succeed in the emotional minefield that is the modern office.

In his influential book on the C++ programming language, Bjarne Stroustrup says that programming is a *human* activity, and *all is lost* if this is forgotten.[1] While I don't know that all is lost if we forget this, I will say that software engineering is a *social* activity, and ignoring this fact is a recipe for career failure.

Software is developed by teams of people working towards a common goal. Projects succeed when team members communicate and cooperate—as if they were in a good marriage. They understand each other and are compassionate and supportive. In-

---

[1] Bjarne Stroustrup, *The C++ Programming Language (2ʳᵈ ed.)* (Addison-Wesley, 1991), p. 363.

terpersonal conflicts introduce delays and inefficiencies, so are best avoided.

If you are reading this book you are likely either preparing to become a software engineer, are already employed as one, or manage a group of them. This book is my take on the social aspects of software engineering—the human factors of programmers. My intent is to inform and entertain with a series of short essays about the personal and emotional issues that affect the quality of life of a software engineer. In particular, if you are a student or new to the field, I hope this book will help you understand:

- the truly important stuff that you learn in university;

- what to expect from the real world in terms of career paths, work environments and politics; and,

- that your talent as a programmer will dictate how far your career takes you, but how well you know your personality strengths and weaknesses will dictate how quickly you get there.

Books like *Winners Never Cheat* and *All I Really Need to Know I Learned in Kindergarten* romanticize the lessons of childhood and attempt to apply them to the problems of adulthood. Since software engineering is a social activity that is rife with politics, intrigue and conflict, one might write a book that suggests that the key to better management of software projects can be found on the playground.

This is not one of those books.

Maybe if my childhood had been different I could have written that book. Reality is more complex than the playground, however, and most of us carry the scars of some pretty harsh lessons with us to work every day. As we shall see, this isn't necessarily a bad thing.

Eminent software engineer Fred Brooks once said that "adjusting to the requirement for perfection is, I think, the most difficult part of learning to program."[2] However, some of us found that adjustment quite painless, especially as new programming tools like the debugger were invented. Adjusting to the imperfections of others is, I think, the most difficult part of learning to be a software engineer. There are no debuggers for people. If you don't appreciate the fact that we are all imperfect humans who wear our injuries on our sleeves, your career goals—not to mention your personal goals—will likely suffer.

The most important lessons you will learn during your career as a software engineer are the personal ones that make you a better human, not the technical lessons that make you a better programmer. Experience teaches us that the personal lessons gleaned through our childhood and adult experiences are key ingredients in the journey to technical maturity.

As someone who tried to balance parallel careers in academia and industry, I know there is a divide between those who teach software engineering and those who practice it professionally. I finally gave up after it became apparent I could not stand tall with one foot on each side of the chasm. I left teaching in 2005 to concentrate on building a startup that would morph into a leading social game studio.

---

[2] Frederick P. Brooks, *The Mythical Man-Month: Essays on Software Engineering* (Addison-Wesley, 1975), p. 8.

The disconnect between academia and industry sometimes causes students to feel detached from their professors (to whom they can't relate), practitioners to lose touch with the results of academic research, and the perception that professors are all whack-jobs who rely on institutional protection for their employment. While I don't pretend that students, professionals, and educators are always on the same page, I do respect the specific roles of each. I have thoroughly enjoyed being all three, and optimistically hope this little book might help to reduce some of the tensions amongst them.

I don't have any quantifiable, peer-reviewed answers to the problems and complexities inherent in building large-scale software systems. However, I do have some anecdotes, observations and plenty of opinions. I am not selling a methodology or a technology, but if I had to distill the essence of what I am selling down to one concept, it is this:

Overcome your insecurities and be nice to your co-workers.

Compassionate understanding and acceptance of oneself and others will make us all better people and better software engineers.

Table of Contents

I, Programmer

In which we introduce the Three Laws of Software Engineering.

When I taught the third year undergraduate course on software engineering at the University of Victoria (UVic), I began by asking students if they could define the topic of study, **software engineering**. Many of my students were in a formal engineering degree program; others were computer science majors within the Faculty of Engineering. Surprisingly, they struggled to offer a satisfactory definition of what it was they were studying.

So we start with engineering, which I take to be the building of useful tools for humanity. It follows that software engineering is the building of useful software tools for humanity. But isn't that just programming? How is software engineering different from computer science?

A common public misconception is that computer scientists design and build computers. Designing computer hardware is actually the job of computer engineers. Computer science is about software: the mathematics of computation, the science of abstraction, and the art of programming. The vast majority of computer science graduates end up in careers as software engineers, writing practical software applications for other people to use.

Fred Brooks suggests that the scientist builds things in order to study, whereas the engineer studies in order to build things.[1] In order to build software systems, the engineer must study computer science. Lots of computer science. Thus the reality is that most practicing software engineers are computer science graduates—not formally trained engineers.

This anomaly led to a minor controversy in North America regarding the use of the title *Engineer* to describe what it is exactly that computer scientists do for a living. In fact, I can probably expect an injunction from one or more of the governing bodies of Professional Engineers for my improper and publicly misleading use of said protected noun throughout this book.

Whatever. The truth is, you wouldn't want to hire any kind of Professional Engineer to create a software tool—they simply don't have the requisite background knowledge. Worse, after they invariably screw it up, they will blame you and tell you how much harder their degree was to complete because they had to take physics. (More about this in later chapters when we discuss the evils of self-taught programmers.)

To summarize:

- Software engineering is the multi-person construction of multi-version software. It is also the name given to the branch of computer science whose research focus is the application of **engineering rigor** to the problem of building large, complex software systems on time and on budget.

---

[1] Frederick P. Brooks, "The Computer Scientist as Toolsmith II," *Communications of the ACM*, 39 (3), 1996, pp. 61-68. He further postulates that by any reasonable criterion, computer science is not a science—it is engineering.

- Software engineers work in project teams. They build programs for other people (the end-user, client, customer, or other software engineers) to use.

- Software engineering is therefore a social activity. Programmers regularly interact with each other, and sometimes (if permitted) with the customer. Good communication, hygiene, and social skills are required.

- Software engineers write small units of code rather than complete programs. Their code is combined with the code of other software engineers to create large, complex programs.

The study of computer science, as a separate discipline, provides software engineers with the knowledge and tools to do their job effectively. A good software engineer needs to know more about computer science than is taught as part of any of the curricula in the traditional electrical, mechanical, and even computer engineering departments.

The definition of software engineering as *the multi-person construction of multi-version software* is generally attributed to David Parnas.[2] He was actually my professor back when I was an undergraduate at UVic. Dr. David Lorge Parnas, the man who in 1972 virtually invented the concepts of information hiding, encapsulation, and abstract interfaces, and thus drew the roadmap of modern best programming practices, was certainly the most famous professor I ever took a course with at UVic. I thought it was pretty cool that twenty years later I was teaching the same course at the same

---

[2] David Parnas, "Software Engineering or Methods for the Multi-Person Construction of Multi-Version Programs," in *Programming Methodology*, Lecture Notes in Computer Science 23 (Springer Verlag, 1975), pp. 225-235.

institution, using a textbook with an entire chapter devoted to his now famous case study in software design (the KWIK index).

Figure 1. David Parnas. Photo by Hubert Baumeister.

My girlfriend at the time I was a student, Lynda, succinctly distilled the entire curriculum of Parnas' class down to one idea: **design for change**. She remarked that he could have saved us a lot of time if he simply had showed up for the first class and apologized for his lack of teaching skill, but explained that it did not matter because all he really had to say was "design for change." He then could have handed over the actual work of instructing us about how to put that idea into practice to his competent graduate student and teaching assistant, Gord Stuart.[3]

David Parnas is undoubtedly a man of great intellect, and one of the most influential professors I have ever met. I still recall the

---

[3] I would later teach with Dr. Stuart at Camosun College. He pretended to remember me.

exact moment when, sitting in the dark programming lab in the basement of the Clearihue Building completing an assignment for his course, I grasped the elegance of using another programmer's code only through its abstract public interface. I know that must sound silly or, like most great ideas, obvious in hindsight. But what my current crop of undergrads liked hearing about wasn't the brilliance of his ideas so much as stories about what kind of professor he was. They wanted to know: *Did Parnas suck?*

I first heard of the legend that is David Parnas while I was on a co-op work term.[4] One of my managers—a jaded, humorous old mainframe programmer at the Ministry of Forests—referred to him as *feisty*, and a sufferer of *little man syndrome*. He also insisted that when I returned to school that I take Parnas' course on software engineering. I was only 20 years old at the time and didn't yet know anything about height, and its effects on the male psyche. Indeed, I can't really say that I noticed people's height at all. Short or not, my take is that Parnas believed that he was right about everything. He simply didn't leave room in his mental universe for other opinions, or for very much else other than solving the world's software engineering problems. He didn't even know who Bobby Orr was, which should have immediately made him ineligible to work in Canada. Despite his repeated use of the punch line "after he regained consciousness" to describe how he dealt with those who dissented with his notion of the one true way to write software, Dr. Parnas' lack of cultural awareness meant that he lacked street credibility with us.

---

[4] A co-op work term is like a paid internship. In the cooperative education model, students alternate semesters at school with semesters on work term placements organized by their university. It took me five years to complete my Bachelor of Science degree at UVic, but I graduated with 20 months of invaluable work experience.

The great irony is that David Parnas wasn't a good team player. While he was a star programmer and an egoist, he was also a man of principle. His resignation from the US Strategic Defense Initiative (SDI, also derisively known as the Star Wars project) was exemplary. He carried a hanky and liked to blow his seemingly always congested nose during his lectures. I think he was slightly autistic. I was afraid of him.

Superficially, the lower middle-class, provincial, Canadian, twenty year old students in his classroom (me included) couldn't relate to him—we didn't know many people who went to high school in the Bronx, or people that worked in Holland with Edsger Dijkstra, or programmers who wrote documentation in first-order logic, or who wrote cockpit software for the US Navy A6 fighter plane. Nor did Professor Parnas seem to worry about relating to us. He never drew on the board or used any visual cues to convey his ideas. Our textbook consisted of a photocopied spiral-bound collection of everything he (and only he) had ever published, much of which we found impenetrable given our lack of intellectual maturity and professional experience.

But despite our immaturity, and unbeknownst to us at the time, David Parnas taught us much of what we would eventually need to know about software engineering. In particular, he laid the foundation for our painless transition from procedural to object-oriented programming. As well, I find myself time and again returning to his concept of the *uses hierarchy* as a means of defining project milestones as subsets of the complete system design.

More importantly, Parnas' definition of software engineering, *the multi-person construction of multi-version software,* tells us both *what* we should do, and *how* we should it. The science of software engineering is all contained in the two *multis* that make up his definition.

The term **multi-person** means that the software is written by a team of programmers. Before any programming begins, the system is designed by decomposition into individual work units called *modules* so that the work can be done in parallel by the members of the team. Modules are independent compilation units in a language like C or classes in an object-oriented language like Java. The team members program their assigned modules, which are then combined to form complete systems.

The term **multi-version** means that the software will change over time. The decomposition of the system into modules is done so that each module hides one design decision behind an abstract interface. The modules interact (call each other) only through these interfaces. Since the public interfaces are less likely to require modification than the private implementations they hide, the complexity of making changes to the software is reduced.

In other words, design for change. Just as Lynda used to say.

Designing for change is such an important concept that I have made it the foundation of what I propose as the *Three Laws of Software Engineering*.

1. A software engineer must design for change.
2. A software engineer must obey orders given by his or her manager, except where such orders would conflict with the First Law.
3. A software engineer must protect his or her own continued employment, even if this conflicts with the First or Second Law.

The First Law is essentially a principle of professional ethics that each of us must strive to maintain.

The Second Law reflects the reality that software engineering is a profession. We trade our time and expertise for money.[5] In most instances, our activities are supervised by managers who do not necessarily share the same set of goals and concerns that we do.

The fact that software engineers face conflicts between the principle of designing for change and the need to remain employed is captured in the Third Law. The *science* of software engineering tells us we should design for change by taking the time to create systems properly, so that they not only meet the requirements, but do so in a way that will make future modifications as painless as possible. The reality is that the software engineer is rarely afforded the time necessary to do it right. Subsequently, the *art* of software engineering is in knowing what corners to cut (and when) in order to ensure that you ship on time, and that your enterprise survives in a market-driven environment. This is especially true for those working in web application development because they will find themselves under constant pressure to release new versions of the code based on the immediate feedback of the customers.

As anyone employed for more than five minutes in our industry can attest, managers are always giving orders that lead to conflict with the First Law. The unending pressure to ship the next release of the software means that the Third Law dominates. Software engineers are often conflicted: they can stick to principles and risk getting fired, or compromise and meet the deadline. Or, as was the case of David Parnas and the SDI committee, one

---

[5] Open source projects aside, though I personally have difficulty with anyone who gives away our service for free... hell, even Doctors Without Borders pays its field staff a stipend.

could resign and accept the career-limiting consequences of that action.

The difference between a seasoned software engineer and a rookie is in the brush strokes of the pro. The experienced software engineer will intuitively know when to violate the First Law, and how to do it in such a way as to minimize the impact of not designing for change on those who will need to refine the source code long after the original engineer has moved on to another project.

End Notes

The three laws and the title of this entry are of course intended to pay homage to the short stories of Isaac Asimov.

David Parnas' seminal paper on how to design programs so they are easier to change, which uses the KWIK index as an example, is "On the criteria to be used in decomposing systems into modules," *Communications of the ACM*, 15 (12), pp. 1053-58.

Dan Hoffman and David Weiss have compiled a *greatest hits* collection of the papers that David Parnas published over the years as *Software Fundamentals: Collected Papers by David L. Parnas* (Addison-Wesley, 2001).

The Lynda I mention was Lynda Wong—a sweet, funny, smart young woman who effortlessly made people smile. It was the spring semester of 1986 when we took CSC365 with David Parnas. We fell out of touch the following year after we broke up, but I was shocked and deeply saddened when I heard of her death from cancer in 2006. I wish I had treated you better, Lynda.

The Software Engineer Life Cycle

Not unlike the software systems they construct, a programmer's productivity also follows a life cycle. While everything software engineers do falls into one of the five categories that comprise the software development life cycle, the effectiveness with which they undertake their tasks is governed by where they are in the software engineer life cycle.

Legendary Canadian businessman Jimmy Pattison was famous for his ruthless policy of firing the poorest performing monthly salesperson at each of his many car dealerships. I could never have done that at Backstage Technologies, the contract software engineering firm that I started in 2005, because excellent programmers are extremely difficult to replace. But that doesn't mean I didn't rule with an iron fist. In fact, I think there could be a Japanese-style TV reality show set at Backstage entitled *Iron Fist*. Each weekly episode of *Iron Fist* would conclude with me, adorned in metal gloves, whaling on the nuts of the employee with the fewest accumulated lines of code in production. Unfortunately, most weeks that would be me.

Why is my productivity waning, and why isn't the amount of work that my employees do consistent? Not unlike the software systems they construct, a programmer's productivity follows a predictable life cycle.

The Software Development Life Cycle

According to Webster, a life cycle is the series of stages through which an individual, culture, or manufactured product passes during its lifetime. In the case of a software product, the usual stages of its life are: requirements, design, implementation, testing, and maintenance.

Briefly, the **requirements** stage is when the product is conceptualized as a set of requirements that are documented by a business analyst. This is *what* the product must do.

The **design** stage is when a software architect imagines how the software will be built. The software architect decomposes the system into a set of interacting subsystems (database server, application server, web server, etc.), which in turn are decomposed into their constituent modules (database tables, transactions, stored procedures, classes, processes, threads, etc.). The architecture of the system is usually described by a set of directed graphs, where the nodes are the subsystems or modules and the arcs denote relationships (e.g., "calls", "stores", "reads"). This is *how* the product will work.

The **implementation** stage involves database administrators and programmers realizing the design as a working program.

The **testing** (or **verification**) stage is meant to ensure that the program meets the requirements. Once this has been determined a version of the program is released to its user community.

Finally, the **maintenance** stage is where the program is changed into new releases that fix bugs that were not discovered during the testing stage, and into new versions that add additional features.

Part of the goal of software engineering is to apply what is known as engineering rigor to the process of programming. The theory is that if it's good for building bridges and toaster ovens, it should work just as well when writing software. Engineers love linear project plans that involve milestones, diagrams, and documents. When this concept was applied to software development it led to the infamous waterfall model of the software development life cycle (see Figure 2). The waterfall model imagines each of the five stages of the life cycle as a self-contained step, where the output of each step falls only into the next. The model does not allow for backtracking or for information to flow in any direction but down. The obvious analogy to shit rolling downhill is left as an exercise to the reader.

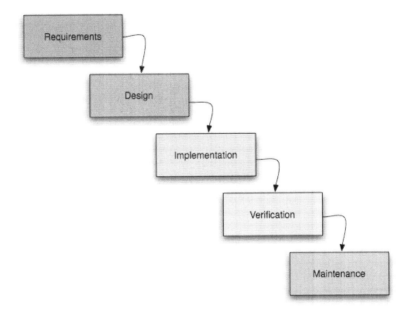

Figure 2. The waterfall model of the software development life cycle. Image by Paul A. Hoadley.

Programmer Productivity

Most textbooks on software engineering make at least passing reference to the notion of programmer productivity. The conventional wisdom is that an average programmer completes a paltry 500 debugged lines of code (LOC) per month. This number seems absurdly low.

The standard set of explanations for the apparent low productivity of working software engineers includes **Brooks' Law** (which states that due to the increased communication overhead of working in teams, adding manpower to a late software project only serves to make it later), and that time is allotted to non-programming activities like requirements gathering, documentation, and design.

These explanations tell only part of the story. While it has long been accepted that productivity rates can differ by an order of magnitude between the best and worst programmers, little has been said regarding the reality that work rates of the *same* programmer can differ over time as well.

The Software Engineer Life Cycle

Programmers follow a predictable productivity life cycle that is directly related to their emotional state. After an initial six month period of intense interest, at which time productivity rates are indeed much higher than the oft-quoted 500 LOC/month average, programmers experience a short period of volatility before they enter a prolonged phase of steadily dwindling interest. It is during this stage of dwindling interest that productivity rates approach the average. Each time a programmer switches employers or begins a significantly new project, the life cycle starts anew.

My experiences and observations while working as the senior software engineer for two successful internet startups (Abe-

Books.com in Canada, then Prophet.Net in the United States) point to the simple conclusion that employees are most productive when interest and satisfaction in their jobs is at its highest.

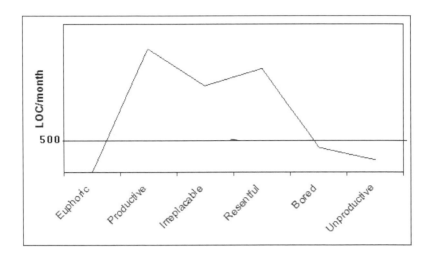

Figure 3. Productivity as a function of stage in the software engineer life cycle.

Everything we do as software engineers falls under one of the five stages that comprise the software development life cycle. The effectiveness with which we undertake these tasks is governed by where we are in the software *engineer* life cycle (see Figure 3).

The software engineer life cycle is comprised of six stages:

1. Euphoric

2. Productive

3. Irreplaceable

4. Resentful

5. Bored

6. Unproductive

While this particular life cycle model is perhaps most likely to apply to highly productive individuals (so-called *star programmers*) who work in the 24/7 world of web development and e-commerce, it is my belief that it contains fundamental truths that apply to many software development situations.

Euphoric. The first stage describes the emotional state of a programmer at the start of a new job or significantly different project. The programmer is stimulated by both the newness of the environment and the challenges ahead. In many cases the programmer's euphoria is also fueled by their coincident escape from a previous work situation that had become routine or was under-utilizing their talents. This introductory phase is quite short and lasts only as long it takes to acclimatize to the new surroundings, learn a new development environment, and become familiar with the application domain.

Productive. Once acclimatized, the programmer's work interest reaches a peak and productivity is at its highest. This stage—which lasts about six months—is when the programmer develops or takes ownership of some mission-critical software system, and coincides with the programmer's steadily rising value to the organization.

These first two stages are the honeymoon period. The next two are best described as the volatility phase.

Irreplaceable. Management soon recognizes that the programmer has become a valuable commodity. Because the programmer's prestige within the organization is at an all-time high, this is the stage at which increases in compensation and fringe benefits are offered in an effort to keep the programmer from ever possibly leaving. The golden handcuffs are sealed with the ubiquitous stock option grant, or the promise of one. The programmer feels on top of the world. Unfortunately this will not last.

Resentful. Management—sensing a sudden shift in the power dynamic common to the employer-employee relationship— begins to resent that a single individual (the programmer) is now responsible for the ongoing success or failure of the venture. Fearing a loss of control, management asserts ownership of the programmer's time and space by requiring the programmer to carry a pager, to work weekends, to install broadband connectivity at home, and to never, under any circumstances, take holidays. The programmer will start to receive email at all hours of the day from trigger-happy monitoring software that reports false alarms, and from managers requesting new features and emergency bug fixes.

In return, the programmer develops feelings of resentment towards management. This is exacerbated by management's policy of rewarding the programmer's competency, not with bonuses and time off, but with additional workload and responsibilities.

This unstable time of mutual resentment is necessarily short-lived, as emotions run too high for the process to carry on for more than a month or two. The working relationship can implode during the resentful stage, particularly if volatile personalities are involved. In the worst case, the programmer quits because the additional workload coupled with the stress of being irreplaceable yet resented becomes too much to take. However, in most cases the resentful stage merely settles into an equilibrium of mutual need: management's need for the star to keep the software running, and the programmer's need to be a star.

Bored. The post-resentment equilibrium sees the programmer's activities shift more towards ongoing maintenance, consultative meetings with management, and internal knowledge transfer to other programmers and customer support staff. Because the initial challenges of the new project, environment, and technologies have all been met, the intellectual stimulation has dropped. This leads to boredom. Coupled with the excessive mental context switching demanded of the new activities, the programmer's productivity (as measured by LOC/month) experiences a significant drop. Despite the tedium, however, this stage can last indefinitely if the programmer's productivity satisfies minimum expectations according to the programmer's current remuneration.

Unproductive. Like a manic depressive who goes off his medicine because he misses the occasional euphoric episode, or a love junkie addicted to the adrenaline rush of the first six months of a new relationship, the programmer is unlikely to remain in a state of boredom forever: something has to give. The slide into the unproductive stage has begun when the programmer starts polishing the resume and visiting job sites on the web. At this stage management views the programmer as coasting, overpriced, and expendable. One of two outcomes is inevitable: the programmer will find a new employer, or management will move the programmer to a significantly new role or project. Either way, the life cycle will start again.

Conclusion

This life cycle model should serve as a cautionary tale to both programmers and managers. The lesson for the programmer is to be aware of each stage and its effect on productivity levels, for ultimately one's success as a software engineer depends on one's perceived productivity. By recognizing the symptoms of boredom leading to unproductiveness, the programmer can proactively search for remedies, usually in the form of a frank discussion with management, or seeking out new projects and technological challenges.

Conversely, managers must understand the causes and effects of this life cycle in order to combat high levels of attrition and declining productivity. To get the most out of the organization's stars, managers must resist the temptation to over-burden irreplaceable programmers with additional responsibilities lest they kill the golden goose with resentment. Instead, managers should look for challenges that will keep their stars performing at peak levels.

End Notes

The waterfall model is from Winston Royce, "Managing the Development of Large Software Systems," *Proceedings of IEEE WESCON 26*, 1970, pp. 1-9. Ironically, Royce proposed the waterfall as an example of how not to build software systems.

The first study to find significant differences in programmer productivity is Sackman, H. H., W. J. Erikson, and E. E. Grant, "Exploratory experimental studies comparing online and offline programming performance," *Communications of the ACM*, 11 (1), 1968, pp. 3-11.

The 500 lines of code per month average is cited in Van Vliet, H., *Software Engineering Principles and Practice (Second Edition)*, John Wiley & Sons, 2000, p. 175.

Brooks' Law is from Frederick P. Brooks, *The Mythical Man-Month: Essays on Software Engineering*, Addison-Wesley, 1975. In this same book, Brooks estimates that good programmers are five to 10 times more productive than ordinary ones.

An earlier version of this essay appeared as "The Programmer Life Cycle," *Software Engineering Notes*, 29 (3), 2004.

Your Favourite Methodology Is eXtremely Gay

Good software is not *an emergent property of the rules that govern the decentralized interactions of average programmers. Instead, good software results from good programmers, regardless of the methodology. Keep your software process from getting in the way of your best programmer.*

When programming, you can never have too many comments. No, wait… when programming, you can never have too many jelly donuts. I always get those confused. The former is an example of a coding standard, which can be part of a programming methodology. The latter is an example of a software development process (albeit one that includes "now we will eat some jelly donuts" as a phase in the life cycle). In this chapter we discuss the difference between a software development process and a methodology, and why neither really matters.

Software Process versus Methodology

In trying to apply engineering rigor to the problem of building large, complex software systems on time and on budget, significant effort has been spent developing formal processes and methodologies that can ensure repeated success in the development of quality software products.

A **software process** is the set of steps, activities, or phases that engineers follow in the development of a software product. The waterfall model of the software development life cycle is an example of a software process. It is common for each step to produce as output a set of deliverables (usually in the form of documents) that are signed-off by an authority. Documenting the phases and having them signed off is known as **visibility**, which is considered an important part of engineering rigor. There are many benefits to being visible, including automatic ass-covering ("but you agreed to this specification...") and having something to give the new co-op students to read for the first few days when they arrive for work and you have nothing prepared for them to do yet.

A **software development methodology** fills in the details of how each activity in the software process should be done. A methodology stipulates what the specific deliverables are, what their format should be, and how they are to be generated. It answers such questions as, how do we capture unambiguous requirements? How should the system be decomposed into modules? How do we document the design? Do we program in pairs or alone? Do we utilize code reviews or unit test?

A methodology is about taking a disciplined approach, whether to making coffee, investing in the stock market, or writing software. In the case of an investment methodology, for example, the goal of the discipline is to increase the likelihood that you will make money even if the majority of your stock picks don't pan out. How? By cutting your losses early and letting your winners ride. Likewise, a good software methodology will serve to help minimize your losses by, for example, catching bugs as early in the process as possible, or by achieving a working system that is easy to change.

To summarize:

- A **software process** identifies the sequence of steps undertaken during the development of a software product. A **visi-

ble software process goes further by defining the documentation produced during each step of the process.

- A **software development methodology** dictates an orderly approach to completing each of the steps identified by the software process.

To further elaborate on these concepts, let us revisit the phases of the waterfall model of the software development process.

Requirements. Stroustrup suggests that knowing what it is you are building is the crucial first step.[1] However, if you have a target audience or pre-existing user community that will provide feedback (quite vocally, I may add), is it really possible to know what you will end up building when you begin? I can't recall any significant software project that I have worked on where we knew ahead of time exactly what the artifact would ultimately become. Unlike many programmers, who see this as a curse, I see the lack of initial requirements for the ultimate goal, and the emergent quality of the process itself, as one of the most compelling reasons to build software rather than consumer products. It is tremendously exciting to work with a medium that is so fluid. While I can see that you wouldn't want to start construction on a condominium tower without first knowing what it was you are trying to build, there is no good reason to assume that such certainty is possible or even necessary with software.

It is annoying when the grouchy programmer insists on clear, complete requirements before design and coding begins. It is a fact of life that requirements will change, so why insist that the

---

[1] Bjarne Stroustrup, *The C++ Programming Language (2nd ed.)* (Addison-Wesley, 1991), p. 362.

specifications exist beforehand? Embrace the chaos: come on in, the turbulence is fine! And if you can't, might I suggest zoloft or effexor as an excellent means of combating anxiety.

Design. The output of the design phase is the **software architecture**, which includes the software components, the externally visible properties of these components, and the relationships amongst these components. For example, in an object-oriented design, the architecture is described by the set of classes (and interfaces), their public methods, and the inheritance, composition, and uses relationships between these classes. Normally the software architecture is described by a directed graph, where the nodes are the classes to be implemented, and the arcs represent the relationships between the classes.

If you don't have the design right you might as well go home. Mistakes in any other phase can be corrected relatively easily after the fact, but redesign is a monumental pain. How do you learn good design? Same as how we humans learn anything: through imitation of others who are good at it, trying it ourselves, and learning from our mistakes. Learning how to design software is like learning to ride a bike: incredibly difficult the first few times you try it, but second nature through repetition and experience.

Implementation. Alec Baldwin in the film *Glengarry Glen Ross*, while delivering probably the best de-motivational corporate speech ever, said it best: "A-B-C. Always Be Coding." At least I think that's what he said. I wasn't really paying attention.

Seriously, though, I think I speak for all software engineers when I say we wish we could always be coding. In the waterfall model, the implementation phase depends upon the design, which depends upon an incomplete and changing set of requirements. We love to program, and part of the thrill and joy of programming comes from the emergence of solutions to problems that could not have been anticipated in the requirements or even design stage.

Testing. In theory, the testing phase of the software life cycle is when the testing team ensures the product meets the requirements. However, **software testing** is not the process of proving a program is correct, or that it meets the specification; it is the process of executing a program with the intention of finding bugs. This definition is founded on the safe assumption that all non-trivial programs have bugs. Proving program correctness is not only impractical, it can bias the way the tester approaches his task. Testing to specifications rather than searching for bugs can lead to products that are not **robust**, crashing the first time they are exposed to an unexpected sequence of inputs.

In any online business, first past the post is a crucial advantage. If you take the time to follow a slow traditional software process, like the waterfall model, you risk failure for the entire enterprise. At AbeBooks.com, we developed our own software process to cut back on the time it took to ship new versions of the website. Its defining feature: the end-users tested the software for us. Everything was in beta, all the time. Eliminating an entire phase of the process was certainly a massive time-saver that helped us maintain our industry advantage.

Don't try this at home: skimping on test is always a bad idea. What saved our ass was that we were better, faster, and cheaper than the competition. That and our complete control over the deployment process enabled us to recover quickly from bone-headed mistakes.

With Alibris nipping at our heels, we didn't have time for code reviews and regression testing at AbeBooks.com. We didn't have

Alibris' bags of venture capital and glossy ad campaigns, either. But what we did have was a team that was wholly invested in the survival of the enterprise, and there was no fucking way we were going to let those assholes beat us.[2] We were there first and worked feverishly to maintain the lead.

Maintenance. Alas, the relentless pressure of constant shipping takes its toll. The term *internet years* is really about their effects on your body: one year of web application development for a startup will age you by five years compared to the six month release cycle employed by shrink-wrap and custom software vendors. Inevitably, bugs will arise in the web app due to unforeseen spaghetti effects and the compressed development cycle (see Figure 4 for a typical software development process at an internet startup).

At Prophet.Net, it was not uncommon for management to ask for a postmortem analysis of why that innocuous change resulted in 18 hours of downtime. This became unnecessary once they adopted what became known as *Russ's Rule:* it is always the database administrator's fault. It became such a time saver in the whole development cycle that it was officially codified into their process workflow template (see Figure 5).

The Problem

Software engineering is unique amongst engineering disciplines in that adherence to accepted methods and a rigorous, visible process does not guarantee success. We have yet to discover any software process and methodology that ensures repeatable results when it comes to developing large complex systems of sufficient quality in a cost effective manner. But in my experience, it's not

---

[2] Competitive people say *fuck* a lot, so expect to hear it more frequently in the workplace as you climb the management ranks.

the methodology or process that is to blame if a software system fails to meet requirements. Rather, the blame lies squarely at the feet of the software engineers who were unable to tackle the complexity of the system under development.

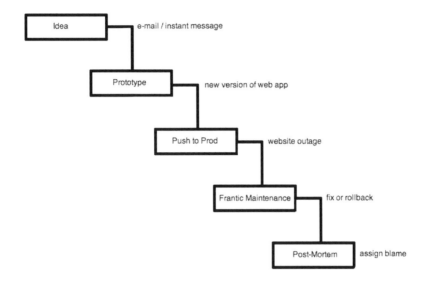

Figure 4. The Prophet.Net software process. At Prophet.Net, the requirements phase consisted of the CEO delivering an idea for a new feature, usually via instant message. The design and implementation phases were combined into rapid prototyping. After a few scrawls on a white board or on the back of a napkin at Starbucks, the coding consisted of some on-the-fly hack, or maybe even a kludge, of existing code. Often a new table was added, or additional columns to existing tables, in the database instance. The programmer would test on his workstation using a local build of the web application and a shared developer instance of the database. When the prototype was ready to be discussed, it was committed to the code repository and pushed to the staging environment so that the CEO could have a look. Once the CEO signed off (usually by barking "ship it!" across the hallway), the new code was pushed to production. Typically this happened about 4:30 PM on a Friday. Without a dedicated quality assurance team, integration testing was left to our end users. When the website fell over under the load of the thousands of customers out

there in the cloud, a panic ensued: "WE ARE DOWN!" If the existing check-ins to the code repository were coherent, and you could find the build manager, the simplest solution would be to rollback to the previous version. However, this was often impossible due to some marketing decision that made progress only possible in the forward direction. During the frantic all-hours weekend maintenance that ensued, the first place to look for the problem would be in the database management system's slow queries log: usually the outage was due to a new index that was present on the test database but missing on the production instance. Monday morning would typically began with a post-mortem meeting to discuss what went wrong and to discuss ways to improve the process to avoid repeating the latest disaster. But before long this meeting would veer off into a brainstorming session regarding ideas for new features, and the process would repeat.

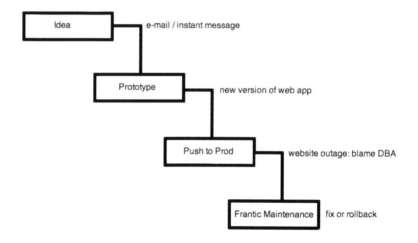

Figure 5. *Russ's Rule* eliminates the need for the post-mortem phase of the Prophet.Net software process. If the web application fails, it is always the fault of the database administrator (DBA).

For example, building a scalable, highly-available web application in a modern programming language like Java is subtly complex. The programmers need to have a strong grasp of concepts such as multi-threaded programming and thread synchronization, caching, database connection pooling, database transactions, and data structure and algorithmic analysis, to name but a few. The complexity of the underlying database management system alone can lead to project failure if someone on the team lacks the requisite knowledge to tune and scale the system through horizontal partitioning (i.e., sharding) as the size of the database grows. The ability of software engineering to overcome these complexities has nothing to do with software process or methodology and everything to do with the intelligence, experience, and judgement of the people on the team.

Conversely, the best software engineers are able to repeat their previous successes regardless of the software development process or methodology they utilize.

This may be our industry's dirty little secret: programmers are not interchangeable commodities.

What to Do?

First, understand that the *weakest link* metaphor does not apply to software development project teams. The team is much stronger than its weakest member. In fact, it is quite the opposite. A software team is only as good as its strongest member. Additional experience, judgement, and talent cannot be manufactured simply from the interactions of the individuals.

Second, understand that the project will succeed if and only if the complexity of the product is within the grasp of at least one member of the team. One star programmer can carry an entire troupe of death marchers on his back and drive the bus for everyone. In this regard, Brooks' Law is not universal: adding the right programmer to a team can save the day if a project is late due to incompetence.

Third, understand that the software process and methodology is irrelevant if the complexity of the product is beyond the grasp of the team. It doesn't matter how many jelly donuts you buy, the software is not going to meet the requirements if the team lacks the skill and experience to produce it. Quality software is not an emergent property of a methodology governing the interactions of average programmers. To paraphrase Brooks, there are no silver bullets, but there are golden programmers.

Despite this predicament, religious adherence to a particular process or methodology remains the opiate of the management. Unfortunately, management's favourite methodologies won't save them from bad programmers, but it will give them something comforting to cling to while the ship is sinking.

End Notes

Brooks has suggested that no single improvement in technology, methodology or management technique would result in a tenfold increase in productivity, but there is a tenfold difference between a great software designer and an average one. See Frederick P. Brooks Jr., "No Silver Bullet—Essence and Accidents of Software Engineering," *IEEE Computer*, 20 (4), pp. 10-19.

My apologies to anyone offended by my pejorative use of the word *gay*. After a long internal debate, I stuck with it for two reasons. First, as homage to the television show *South Park*. Second, because there is something about programming in pairs as advocated by the eXtreme Programming (XP) methodology that I find peculiarly homo-erotic, not unlike mixed martial arts. Not that there's anything wrong with that.

White Trash Software Engineer

Building large software products is not easy. If you want to persevere long enough to be successful at it, I have found that it helps if you were raised with conditional love, fear failure, and lack self-esteem.

My mom's favourite cinematic moment is the scene from *An Officer and a Gentlemen* when Richard Gere, with newly minted officer's commission and freshly-pressed white uniform, marches across the factory floor to sweep Debra Winger off her feet. The film ends with the promise of a life of love and romantic adventure for Winger's character as she follows her man through a series of exotic overseas air force postings. My mother's fondness for this film is likely because it mirrors her own revisionist take on events leading to her marriage to my father. The only problem is that my dad—a budding Sapper in the Canadian Military Engineers—sabotaged his commission when he told his commanding officer to *fuck off* during his officer training in Wainwright, Alberta. As a result, love lifted mom and dad up where they belonged, which was apparently the same place they had started from: Chilliwack (see Figure 6).

So it was that I came to be born in a small but picturesque army town, mostly comprised of three distinct socioeconomic groups: the fundamentally religious, the native Indians, and the white trash. None of these labels particularly fit me like a glove, but through a process of elimination, I gravitated to the latter. My parents listened to Elvis (*Aloha from Hawaii* on 8-track as we drove around in our AMC Gremlin). My mom made hamburger stew every Saturday night, which we ate on TV trays while watching *Hockey Night in Canada*. My Dad never did buy me that mini-bike I always wanted because he spent too much money on cigarettes. Meanwhile, my mom spent most of her time wishing her children were more attractive. Even though I know I shouldn't have taken this personally, since her fixation on my appearance was really just her way of dealing with the pain of being married to my narcissistic father, I can't help but feel that I'm being judged by how I look, and that if I was only a little better looking I'd be more successful.

Figure 6. Chilliwack, British Columbia, Canada is located an hour's drive east of Vancouver in the Fraser Valley. Photo courtesy City of Chilliwack.

None of my immediate nor extended family ever went to university, including my grandparents, whose opportunities for social mobility were yanked out from under them when their parents decided they wanted to be farmers in Western Canada. Instead of continuing as solicitors in London or enjoying a leisurely retirement in Yorkshire, the romantic call of the Canadian frontier (circa 1920) altered my family's trajectory for at least two generations.

I grew up a latchkey kid in a working class subdivision. The homes were new, but nobody could really afford them without both parents working. As a result, the children of my neighbourhood enjoyed a significant amount of unsupervised play, especially during summer vacation when we often played road hockey as long as there was daylight. Without anyone around to cook for us, we ate a lot of Alpha-getti for lunch. In hindsight, at least one of my friends was sexually abused, and it was probably the one that kept suggesting we play "naked games" with him.[1]

Recently it has become popular to bemoan the lack of unstructured and unmediated time that today's children get to explore nature and to be themselves. But we all know what happens when you leave a bunch of white kids unsupervised for very long: Piggy gets killed. *Lord of the Flies* was re-enacted in some bastardized fashion on a daily basis in our suburban playground.

At this point, dear reader, you are probably wondering how a rambling personal memoir is going to help you learn anything about software engineering. To be honest, so am I, except for this nagging feeling I have that a working class background coupled with low self-esteem is the recipe for the ideal software engineer. So bear with me for at least one more paragraph.

---

[1] If out of curiosity and a need for acceptance I decided to join in, that doesn't make me a pervert or gay, does it?

I was raised under the black cloud of a Protestant work ethic and just enough physical abuse to ensure that I never wanted to disappoint any authority figure, especially my father. The male role models that surrounded me were from a generation that came of age during a time of unprecedented economic growth and opportunity in North America, which meant they could be and do pretty much whatever they wanted. Unfortunately it seems that many of my father's generation aspired to become raging, violent, racist homophobes incapable of sensitivity or showing any sign of weakness. But they sure had high standards for us boys, and rarely hesitated to let us know when we were out of line or not measuring up. This was especially true of the vein-bulging hot heads who coached our hockey and baseball teams; the principal who picked children up by the ears; the father who chased his son around the yard slowly insisting that he "come here... come here..." so he could beat him with his belt in front of all of his friends; the uncles that molested our cousins; and so on. Ladies and gentlemen, the Silent Generation—silent, but deadly.

Ultimately these stoic men made me feel vulnerable and weak. (Either that, or it was the abundance of Kraft Dinner I ate, combined with my undiagnosed lactose intolerance.) Subsequently, girls made me feel inadequate (because I saw myself as vulnerable and weak). But man, did I ever refuse to lose, channeling all that anger and misunderstanding and disappointment into a competitive, guilty, fearful, responsible ball of anxiety and intellectual fury. As a result, I was not always a nice kid. And when you're not always a nice kid... well, in my day that meant you would often end up in a fight on the playground—usually in retaliation for some intellectual bullying I was engaged in, but sometimes for merely being in the wrong place at the wrong time.

I was a skinny kid, and more often than not I would lose these fights. Perhaps it is due to this experience that I grew into an adult about whom people have often remarked "he has an edge to him." But I think (hope?) it is a good edge; trust me, you want people on your programming team who got beat up as children, for they will go the extra mile to please those in charge and to prove them wrong. You need someone like me: a white trash software engineer who can turn his hidden injuries of class into advantages that will ensure his team ships on time and on budget. By making sure your team has at least one white trash software engineer, you greatly increase the odds of success.

Why? Consider the alternative: a team of well-heeled, secure individuals who were raised with unconditional love, whose only punishment they knew growing up was nurture and compassion. These are great citizens, and make for ideal friends and neighbours, but would you want to go to war with them? I think not. Given the often Herculean effort required to tackle the complexity of writing software that works, it can be difficult to get these people to devote the necessary mental energy and commitment simply because they don't really give a shit if things don't work out. "There's a bug in my latest check-in...? Oh well. I have to leave early as a friend is coming in from Zurich and she wants to join our run group this evening." Awesome.

I don't want that person on my team. Instead, I want the people that are afraid of failure and are intimate with conditional love. Do not confuse *conditional love* with *tough love*. Tough love says to you, "I am here for you, but not if you continue to act in a self-destructive manner—I won't enable you to do that." Tough love is an actual act of love.

Today, I always feel that my employer loves me conditionally. In particular, they love me when I'm writing exceptional software, and they withhold that love or even hate me when someone finds a bug in it. If you have people who were raised with conditional love on your programming team, they will go the extra mile, but only if they perceive the manager as the person (usually their father or mother... whomever was the alcoholic) in their life who withheld love. If it is safe to disappoint your manager, then you will. If it is not, you won't... and you will always ship on time and on budget, regardless of whether it kills you.

End Notes

In an effort to belittle, manipulate, and control me, my ex-wife (who is affectionately known as my *fucking* ex-wife) used to refer to me as "white trash." I owe the title of this essay to her, even though when I mentioned that I wanted to write a book with this title years ago, she admonished me and suggested that I "rise above." I will leave the rising above to our children, for I own the title, I embrace it, and I love that piece of it which is true while rejecting those parts of it that are not.

What the *Bleep* Should We Know!?

You can work for me if you can answer one simple question.

David Parnas was once asked what he thought was the most often overlooked risk in software engineering. His answer was "incompetent programmers.... One bad programmer can easily create two new jobs a year. Hiring more bad programmers will just increase our perceived need for them. If we had more good programmers, and could easily identify them, we would need fewer, not more."[1]

That was harsh. As usual, though, he is correct.

At this point in my life I think I must have interviewed over 300 candidates for various positions in software development. I have hired dozens of co-op students, and made the hiring decisions on countless permanent positions. I have also fired three people. I only had employees at Backstage from 2005 to 2010, so why all this experience in hiring and firing? Somewhere early on in my career it became known that I was good at the difficult job of appraising the technical skills of applicants. Because of this skill, my

---

[1] Nancy Eickelmann, "ACM Fellow Profile: David Lorge Parnas," *ACM SIG-SOFT Software Engineering Notes*, 24 (3), 1999.

previous employers asked me to become intimately involved in the process of assessing the talent of potential employees.

My technical screening interview consists of a twenty minute conversation where I attempt to verify that the applicant is competent, and that his or her resume is, in fact, truthful. Depending on the position we were hiring for, I had managed to boil the interview down to one simple question—answer it, and you could work for me. It was rather disheartening how many computer scientists were unable to answer it correctly.

The technical screening interview has evolved into something distinct from the normal human resources (HR) style interview. Back when I was a co-op student in the mid-1980s, the interview training we received emphasized those tricky personality questions that all HR people ask: *what are you most proud of?* or *what do you think is your biggest flaw?* And rightly so, as most of the interviewers were HR professionals rather than programmers. The lack of technical questions in HR interviews in those days may have been based on the assumption that the stringent requirements for entry to the optional co-op programme assured potential employers of the technical competence of the applicant. But the demanding entry requirements for co-op programmes have been relaxed over the years. The industry's voracious appetite for more and more software engineers in the time leading up to the dot-com bubble, and the trend towards making co-op a mandatory component of many engineering programmes, meant that those early standards of technical competence could not be sustained.

In my day, the university did the technical screening on behalf of the employers. As times changed, graduation requirements became diluted, and more and more people entered the industry due to the inflated salaries and the potential of overnight millions through stock option plans. The technical quality of so-called software engineers started to vary dramatically, and so the need to screen applicants based on their programming acumen arose.

Great Moments in Technical Screening Interviews

Whether it is my perception that degree requirements have been diluted, or that my standards are simply too high, I believe that many recent graduates lack the skills to program effectively. Here are some hi-lights from a recent round of interviews that I conducted. I'll start with the magic question.

Me: What is the average lookup time, in big-O notation, for an object in a hash table?

Applicant: log-n?

Me: No, that's for a binary search tree. How about for an unsorted linked list, or an array?

Applicant: …n-log-n??

Me: That's for sorting, with a recursive divide and conquer algorithm like merge sort. Try again, without guessing.

Applicant: I didn't really like that class on complexity theory.

Me: Okay, let me put it another way. Give me an example of a problem you solved in Java by using the Hashtable class, and tell me why it was the appropriate choice of data structure?

Applicant: I don't really like using the Hashtable. Vector is much better.

Me: Do you want more coffee? I could sure use some.

For the interested reader, the lookup time for a hash table is $O(1)$, or constant time, assuming you have more buckets than objects, and that your hash function distributes uniformly. More precisely, it is $O(1 + n/b)$ where b is the number of buckets in the hash table and n is the number of objects you want to store. For an unsorted list, the lookup time is $O(n)$, since you can expect to search through half of the list on average.

Why is this important? Clearly, at the very least, a software engineer should know how to choose the correct data structure and algorithms to implement a software solution. Data structures and algorithms are the basic building materials of our profession; choose incorrectly, and the foundation of the application will be compromised as the hardware is forced to work unnecessarily hard while running your code. In the same way that we assume a civil engineer will know when to use bricks and mortar rather than steel reinforced concrete, our clients will assume that a software engineer will know which data structure to use if it is important, for example, that the data be efficiently retrieved in sorted order.

It is for this reason that I hire based on academic performance, using the transcript as an initial high-pass filter. At Backstage, my VP of Technology and my Director of Operations were both former students of mine who were at the top of their classes. For the same reason that I did not entrust my eye surgery to a dentist, I also tried not to hire self-taught programmers or software engineers with a degree in something other than computer science. The problem with being self-taught is that you don't know what you don't know. Self-taught programmers tend to naively underestimate the complexity of things like database transaction control, thread safety, and memory management. This is compounded by the Java programming language, which encourages a naïve use of threads and hides the details of memory management.

The Problem with Java

I firmly believe that we learn from our mistakes. This is especially true when we learn to program. But because Java was designed to prevent common programmer mistakes, particularly those dealing with memory allocation, pointer de-referencing, and array indexing, novice programmers can't learn anything programming in Java. Not that I dislike Java—far from it. I believe that it encapsulates much of the great ideas we have developed in software engineering. I am simply suggesting that if Java is the only imperative language you know, you should pick up a book on C and become friends with the *malloc* and *free* functions. Any text that can teach you to avoid writing a function that returns a pointer to a local array will suffice.

Let me reiterate.

- We learn from our mistakes.
- Java is designed to prevent programmer mistakes.
- Therefore, you shouldn't learn to program in Java.

Case in point...

Me: In Java, under what condition might you expect to see a runtime StackOverflowError?

Applicant: When you push too many things onto a Stack, which is a collection class.

This answer represents a significant lack of experience regarding the von Neumann architecture and the machine that actually runs the code. Each executing program is allocated a runtime stack by the operating system, which is used by the program to pass parameters when function/method calls are made at runtime. It is a stack because the arguments are *pushed* on before the call, and *popped* off upon return. This topic is typically covered in any course on assembler programming, compiler construction, or programming languages, which the applicant should have taken when at school. With that reminder, it should be obvious to the reader that the correct answer is a recursive method without a base case.

Applicant: I never did like recursion.

Me: What do you mean you never did like recursion?

My favourite all-time computer science professor, Dr. Bill Wadge (inventor of, among other things, the Lucid programming language and *Wadge degrees*), once told his class that being comfortable with mathematics and recursion is what separates the humans from the apes when it comes to software expertise. Today, I would add that a working knowledge of the von Neumann machine, memory management, and thread synchronization are as important.

Further compounding the difficulty of finding properly qualified software engineers is that the open source movement and its over-engineered general purpose solutions to such problems as object persistence in relational databases has inadvertently dumbed-down our programmers. I know to say this may be anathema to open-source zealots, but I have the sense that open-source software is killing our profession. While the programming has been left to a few high priests willing to work for free, the rest of us have been reduced to editing XML configuration files until the desired behaviour is observed, but without any real understanding of how or why. Software development using open-source tools has largely become the behavioural study of other people's programs: prod, observe, repeat. As such, we are in danger of training a generation of software engineers who are merely *configuration* engineers. They high-five each other if they get the "Hello, world" JSP to display in their browser, but they wouldn't be able to debug their way out of a class cast exception, even if their jobs depended on it.

Regarding those high-fives… remember, you are supposed to be able to get programs working, so don't act like it's never happened before when you get your program debugged.

The Devil is in the Details

The one important attribute of a potential employee that I would screen for, if I knew how, would be attention to detail. Programmers with a strong sense of attention to detail will complete their work assignments according to the specification rather than when they simply think it is done.

Computer software is merciless in its demands upon attention to detail. Tiny errors propagate, leading one to conclude that everything counts in large amounts.[2] Therefore, programmers need to test their code to at least the point where another programmer won't find a glaringly obvious bug after using it for thirty seconds. Programmers who can't (or won't) effectively test their own code will suck the energy out of a team.

---

[2] Yes, that was a Depeche Mode reference.

The argument that "I'm a big picture kind of guy!" is crap. Computers don't care about the big picture.

In my experience, there is a huge difference between having an idea and implementing it, and that difference is directly related to *attention to detail.* The ability to finish a project depends upon how effectively one can see, prioritize, and juggle the details that go into debugging a large software system. Not everyone is naturally good at detail, and if I could devise a way to teach an eye for detail, I would.

End Notes
The title of this essay is motivated by the controversial film *What the* Bleep *Do We Know!?*

If you want to see Java generate a runtime StackOverflowError, compile and run the following program.

```
public class OverflowMe
{
   public static int recursesMe(int x){
   // there is a missing base case here
      return recursesMe(x-1);
   }
   public static void main(String args[]){
      int x = recursesMe(10);
   }
}
```

While syntactically correct, there is something fundamentally flawed with the following C function, meant to create and initialize an array of integers with the *int* passed as an argument.

```
int* createArray(int n)
{
    int a[128], i;

    for (i=0; i < 128; i++)
        a[i] = n;
    return a;
}
```

I mention it because I have seen programmers make this kind of mistake far too frequently (usually with character strings, which are also often left un-terminated). This function returns a pointer to a local variable: a block of memory within the process stack, which will be overwritten the next time the executing program passes parameters to a function. What you meant to do was this:

```
int* createArray (int n, int size)
{
    int *a, i;
    a = (int*) malloc(sizeof(int) * size);

    if (a != NULL)
        for (i=0; i < size; i++)
            a[i] = n;
    return a;
}
```

...and then clearly document that the caller is responsible for verifying the return value is not NULL, and later freeing the memory allocated for the array. Make friends with *malloc*.

Nobody Ever Got Laid For Buying IBM Equipment

Where are all the babes? The dearth of women in our industry is examined from the perspectives of the female reproductive imperative and the systematizing male brain hypothesis.

I chose to major in computer science for two reasons: money, and I was good at it. As a teenager in the early 1980s, everyone kept telling me "computers—now that's where the future is headed!" and "computers is where the good jobs will be!" I felt a bit like Dustin Hoffman's character in *The Graduate*, only *computers* had displaced *plastics* as the one word to remember. While I didn't end up seduced by a cougarific Mrs. Robinson, I did notice that the advertised salaries for computer programmers in the weekly careers section of the *Vancouver Sun* would invariably make my girlfriend very horny. The promise of lots of money was getting me lots of honey.

But to be honest, I really wanted to be a physicist with expertise in acoustics so that I could grow up to design concert halls. However, in my first semester at university I got a D in physics and an A in computer science, and my path was chosen. Since people like to do what they are good at, and since I am people, I stuck with computer science. It was a good fit for me because I enjoyed it, and it seemed incredibly easy. If there was ever an academic pursuit that was uniquely designed for the way my brain worked, it was computer science.

I once asked my class at Camosun College why they had chosen to major in computer science. This was the year 2001, and I had become slightly exasperated with trying to teach data structures and algorithms to a group of adults who did not seem to share my love for the topic. Indeed, many of my students were only there because the job prospects had seemed so promising just two years earlier. The best response I received to the question was from a young man sitting in the back row, who sarcastically exclaimed "I'm here for the babes!"

Why are there so few women in computer science? For many universities throughout North America, this seems to have replaced *does* $P = NP$ as the single greatest research challenge facing computer science departments. I respectfully submit this essay as my take on the situation. Cautiously, and without judgement, I think there are two leading causes:

1. the lack of attractive male mating partners in our industry is at odds with women's biological imperative for reproduction: women are just not attracted to repressed, unkempt, socially awkward, high-functioning nerds; and,

2. computer science is particularly suited to those endowed with a systematizing brain, which women tend not to have, but is usually found in men—especially the repressed, unkempt, socially awkward, high-functioning nerds.

Taken together, these two reasons conspire to ensure that women choose not to pursue careers as software engineers.

The Female Reproductive Imperative and the Search for Jake Ryan

In a time when women are equally represented in Canadian medical schools and law faculties,[1] why has female enrollment in computer science actually declined since its peak in 1985? Why do female undergraduates choose not to major in our discipline despite the excellent career prospects?

Some of the best computer scientists I have known are women. But that is a bit like saying some of the best hockey players I have known are black. I say this only to point out that women can excel at computer science in its current form, but for some reason, choose not to. The possible causes of this gender imbalance have been debated *ad nauseam* (just google "women in computer science debate" and you'll see what I mean), but no one has come out and suggested that one reason might be the lack of suitable mating options a young woman can expect to meet in our profession.

Let me put it another way. If we want more women to become software engineers, we need more men like Jake Ryan majoring in computer science, and fewer Farmer Teds, Duckies, and Long Duk Dongs.[2] We know from experience, anecdotal evidence, and

---

[1] In 2007, according to the Law School Admission Council, there were more women enrolled in Canadian law schools than men. Likewise for Canadian medical schools, where according to the Canadian Medical Association women accounted for 58% of total enrollment in 2004.

[2] Jake Ryan is Molly Ringwald's love interest in the 1984 John Hughes film *Sixteen Candles*, whereas Farmer Ted is the rebuked geek and Long Duk Dong is the Chinese exchange student. Duckie is the slightly less-geeky but likewise rebuked male friend to Molly Ringwald's starring role in the 1986 John Hughes-penned film *Pretty in Pink*. I am definitely a slightly awkward Duckie kind of guy, and most of my friends in university were Long Duk Dongs and Farmer Teds. In fact, when *Pretty in Pink* first came out, people kept telling me

from several television seasons of *Average Joe* that women don't go for the nerdy guys (unless the guy just had an extreme make-over), so the fact that "you would be the one girl for every five guys!" is not exactly a selling feature to entice women into the field. Society tells us that computer scientists are geeks, and engineers are assholes. Software engineers must therefore be geeky assholes. Given that, why would a woman place herself in a group that is universally perceived as unattractive and unappealing? If a young woman is insecure about the way she looks (and who isn't at the age of eighteen), then why choose to train for a career that is associated with unkempt nerds.

Let us also not ignore the influence of the young woman's mother, whose primary fixation from the age of 50 onward seems to be the impending arrival of grandchildren. Does the mother ever say to her daughter "I wish you would marry a nice computer scientist!" Doctor or lawyer, yes, but not computer scientist. "My grandchildren will be dorks!" she screams in horror to her friends. Does having a daughter studying to become a computer scientist make mom happy, or would she rather that her daughter find a more feminine occupation, like artist, teacher, or nurse? Nursing would be ideal, she muses, because nursing provides a great opportunity for her daughter to meet a nice young doctor. Winning the approval of their mothers, and dealing with the hidden pressures of their mom's own insecurity about their looks might well subconsciously steer women away from careers in computer science.

---

that I had to see this movie because "there is a guy that looks just like you in it." Of course, I assumed they meant Andrew McCarthy, who played the love interest. To my horror, they meant Jon Cryer in the role of Duckie, a resemblance to which I vehemently denied until he resurfaced on television years later in *Two and a Half Men* bearing a striking resemblance to how I remember my own father used to look.

Figure 7. This typical software engineer is a genuine pussy magnet.

While I still have the conch, and tread tenuously the ground of sexual stereotypes, may I be so bold as to give the young male computer scientist some advice regarding the topic at hand. If we want more women to join us in the lab, then we need to make the environment more conducive to engaging social activity. In case you haven't heard, women apparently have a fetish for two things: height and good footwear. Therefore, if we can't have more Jake Ryans, what computer science needs is more tall men with good footwear.

If you are a software engineer and Figure 7 looks like what you see in the mirror, try starting your day with a shower. Wear deodorant, get some contact lenses, stand up straight, lose the pony tail, shave off the facial pubes, and buy some decent shoes. If you aren't sure what to say to a girl, ask her a question about her interests and her family. Take that hot girl you've been in love with since ninth grade (but who only wants to be your friend) on a shopping trip and get her advice on some shoes. But be careful she isn't cock-blocking and out to sabotage your chances with other women by putting you in some chick-repellent footwear. Just because she doesn't want to sleep with you doesn't necessarily mean she wants any other girl to have you, either. You might be her backup plan, but only if you manage to grow into your body, mature a bit, and get laser eye surgery. Though to be honest, she's probably desperate to help you hook up with someone else—so you'll stop stalking and harassing her.

The Extreme Male Brain Hypothesis

It has been suggested that in order to be a really good programmer, it helps if you're a little bit autistic (even so far as suffering from Asperger's syndrome).[3] In his groundbreaking 1944 study of autistic children, Hans Asperger identified a pattern of behavior and abilities in his subjects that included "a lack of empathy, little ability to form friendships, one-sided conversation, intense ab-

---

[3] Steve Silberman, "The geek syndrome," *Wired*, 9 (12), 2001, discusses the tendency of computer scientists and engineers to exhibit autistic traits (in particular, Asperger's syndrome), and the strange cluster of autistic children born from couplings of techies in the Silicon Valley.

sorption in a special interest, and clumsy movements." I don't know about you, but that sounds like a lot of my coworkers. It turns out that autism, strongly genetic in origin, is a condition that is four times more likely to effect boys than girls.[4] Does that mean boys are on average four times more likely to develop brains that are well suited to the attention to detail, focus, and mental arithmetic required to be a good computer scientist? Now *there's* a good mating candidate—an autistic male obsessed with computers.

Recently, psychologist Simon Baron-Cohen of Cambridge has studied the difference between the female and male brains in terms of empathizing versus systematizing. Baron-Cohen's thesis is that due to exposure to testosterone *in utero*, more males than females have systematizing brains, and more females than males have empathizing brains. He even goes so far as to categorize Asperger's as a symptom of an "extreme male brain."

Computer science (and software engineering in particular) is largely about building systems, and thus it follows that having a brain biased towards systematizing should make it easier to learn the skills necessary for success. If Baron-Cohen is correct, certain prevalent paradigms are a predictable by-product of a male way of looking at the world. For example, the relational data model and object-oriented programming are systematic views of the world. They represent domains as entities (objects) that are re-lated to each other in strict taxonomies of inheritance (the "is-a" relationship) and composition (the "has-a" relationship). It's not that the empathizing brain can't or won't think of the world that way, but that it isn't particularly interested in seeing the world in

---

[4] S. Ehlers and C. Gillberg, "The Epidemiology of Asperger syndrome. A total population study," *Journal of Child Psychology and Psychiatry*, 34 (8), pp. 1327-1350.

such patterns. Baron-Cohen would argue that the idea of normal-izing a data model that captures the entities of a particular appli-cation area would be a big yawn for most women.

Perhaps the paradigms that dominate our pedagogy and industry resonate with brains that are more systematizing than empathiz-ing. Declarative programming and its reliance on temporal, se-quential execution; iteration and recursion as control; contiguous, linked data structures; entity-relationship modeling; object-oriented decomposition; communicating sequential processes; context-free grammars; and the von Neumann architecture are all models that are more suited to systematizing brains.

Historically, due to social constraints regarding acceptable roles for women, most of the early practitioners of computing were men. (Grace Hopper, who was particularly adept at navigating societies normally the exclusive domain of men, is the notable exception.) These pioneers of computer science developed the roadmap for the discipline by imposing their particularly systema-tizing male-brained models onto the young science. And over time, these paradigms were reinforced into even more systematiz-ing models that further appealed to male brains. If trends con-tinue, it is possible that this systematizing bias will reinforce itself further, and increasingly alienate women. It certainly could ac-count for the reduction in female enrollment since the peak in 1985, which coincides with the move towards a more systematic approach to software engineering.

Ultimately, if we want more women in computer science we might have to change the science into something that the empa-thizing brain finds more compelling. But then it may not be computer science any more, at least not the traditional discipline that evolved from the von Neumann architecture. Perhaps a different foundation would have led to a more gender neutral set of systems, models, and abstractions.

Why Do We Care?

Despite the fact that the socio-economic barriers that prevented women from entering the traditional male disciplines such as medicine and law have broken down, and despite our best paternalistic efforts to promote the field and to encourage women to major in computer science, they are choosing not to. Why isn't that okay with everyone?

If gender balance in every profession is so important, where are the initiatives to get more men in nursing? Where is the hand-ringing and teeth gnashing about the lack of men in social work? My local university funds a *Women in Engineering and Computer Science* office, but not a *Men in Nursing* office with a mandate to convince the Nursing faculty to change their teaching methods or to promote careers in nursing to young men who would otherwise face undue economic hardship as lifetime sandwich artists at Subway. Ironically, I know an excellent database administrator who left the IT industry after the dot-com meltdown in order to become a nurse because he felt the career prospects were better. Not to mention that overtime was paid, and he no longer had to carry a pager.

If people are not concerned about a gender imbalance in the logging industry, or in diesel mechanics, where the work suits the male physique, why should we try to correct a similar gender imbalance in software engineering, where the work suits an uber male systematizing brain? It used to be explained to me that female participation in the profession was important because we had a serious shortage of skilled workers, and women would help fill the vacancies—but that was before the dot-com meltdown and offshore outsourcing. That argument is now moot. While I would encourage both men and women to major in computer science because I want everyone to enjoy a rich, satisfying and lucrative career, the fact is, women just don't apply.

When I wrote the outline for this essay I was sitting poolside at an exquisite hotel on the Indian Ocean in Dar es Salaam. I was able to afford to be there largely because I had chosen to study computer science—and I want my daughters to enjoy the same freedom and luxuries afforded me by my career choice. But I also want them to be happy with their work and to feel respected for what they do. The most respected, socially mobile, and highest paid professionals in Canada are doctors and lawyers. There is no gender imbalance in these professions any more, which coincidentally also offer opportunities to practice empathy and improve the human condition. So while women are well aware that computer scientists are well paid, they seem to prefer these other occupations that are also well remunerated. Oh, and the guys that major in law and medicine tend to be hotter…and from wealthier families, too.

If it is valid to say that men are not interested in careers in nursing because their brains are not wired to empathize and nurture, and it is okay to let men make their own choices regarding occupations they wish to pursue, then is it not valid to say that women are not wired to care about building software systems and are equally capable of making their own career choices?

End Notes

The title of this essay is an allusion to the old adage that "nobody ever got fired for buying IBM equipment," which IBM used as part of its *fear, uncertainty, and doubt* marketing tactic. The purchase of an IBM solution was the safe choice, despite the fact their mainframe and mini-computers exhibited the aesthetic grace of a washing machine and the elegance of an 8-track tape player. But such is hindsight. One day we all become victims of hindsight. I can hardly wait to look ignorant, misguided, and blamed for all the problems of the future. I am especially looking forward to the day that Bono becomes victimized by hindsight.

Does P = NP is an open research question in theoretical computer science. The question asks whether those problems whose solutions can be efficiently verified by a computer are equivalent to those that can be efficiently solved by a computer.

The April 17, 2007 issue of the *New York Times* includes an article by Cornelia Dean ("Computer Science Takes Steps to Bring Women to the Fold") that discusses the declining enrollment figures of women in computer science since a peak of 38% occurred in 1985. Today the figure is closer to 17%. I actually taught two sections of SENG130 at the University of Victoria in 2004 where the female enrollment was zero. (Yet I still managed to get some hot tamales on Rate My Professor!)

The effect that Jake Ryan had on Gen-X women is discussed by Hank Stuever in an article entitled "Real Men Can't Hold a Match to Jake Ryan of *Sixteen Candles*" that appeared in the February 14, 2004 edition of the *Washington Post*.

What is it with computer scientists and pony tails? Writing software isn't magic, and we are not wizards, hippies, nor shamans. A female project manager once confided in me her belief that all those programmers with pony tails were obviously attempting to compensate for their small penises. But then she drove a Jeep. What is it with project managers and Jeeps?

Some have argued that women turn their backs on computer science because there are not enough positive female role models in the computer science faculty of their schools. Many departments specifically recruited female faculty to hopefully rectify this situation. The result: we now have several universities where the gender ratio of the faculty is completely at odds with the gender ratio of the undergraduates they serve. At Tufts University for example, more than half the faculty are women, but female enrollment has hovered around 20% for the past dozen years. Maybe the quality of the female role models themselves needs improvement; i.e., more Molly Ringwalds and fewer Molly Shannons.

Simon Baron-Cohen wrote an August 8, 2005 article for the *New York Times* ("The Systematizing Brain") that discusses the difference between systematizing and empathizing brains. See also his text *The Essential Difference: Men, Women and the Extreme Male Brain* (Allen Lane, 2003).

Nerdy geniuses—along with comedians and art thieves—are considered *omega heroes* by neuroscientists Ogi Ogas and Sai Gaddam in their groundbreaking study of sexual attraction, *A Billion Wicked Thoughts* (Dutton, 2011), p. 119. Unfortunately, as they succinctly put it, ladies prefer alphas.

All We Really Need To Know about Software Engineering Is in the Film *Office Space*

There are six important lessons in the plot line and characterizations found in the film Office Space that make it mandatory viewing for any software engineer.

One of the difficulties I had with teaching software engineering to a class of undergraduates with very little industrial programming experience was explaining why some of the material was relevant and important. For example, the importance of designing for change is difficult to explain to students who have never experienced the joy and frustration of maintaining a program written by someone else. Because I felt I was unable to teach my students everything they would need to know about software engineering, after waving my arms emphatically in front of the chalk board for twelve weeks, I would screen the film *Office Space* on the last day of class.

The 1999 Mike Judge comedic film, *Office Space*, chronicles the efforts of software engineer Peter Gibbons to find peace with the role of work in his life. One of the few artifacts of popular culture to feature a software engineer as the protagonist (Douglas Coupland's novel *Microserfs* is another), *Office Space* contains many subtle gems of wisdom regarding the craft of software engineering. In particular:

- design for change;

- software engineering is a social activity;

- an untested program does not work;

- not everyone gets to write video games;

- Brooks' Law; and,

- you will be expected to work long hours.

Design for Change

We are all taught as undergraduates that maintenance is the dominant phase of the software development life cycle. As such, our responsibility as software engineers is to design systems that are easy to modify or fix without introducing new bugs; that is, to design for change.

Office Space is set in 1999, at a fictitious Dallas computer firm called Initech, where Peter, like most software engineers, is employed maintaining an existing software system. In particular, Peter is busy fixing Y2K bugs in bank software. The Y2K problem—the need to fix or replace by December 31, 1999 any software system that represented dates using only two digits for the year—is now part of history, but many of us in the industry have forgotten about the incredible effort that software engineers expended fixing all that broken code. The film is an object lesson in how not to design systems, for the code was broken only because the original programmers did not design for change. The film is also a historical reminder of what the Y2K bug was all about, even if Peter's attempt to explain it to his love-interest Joanna is aborted when he senses her waning interest.

That the Y2K "crisis" ultimately was an anti-climactic non-event suggests the scope of the problem was severely overestimated by industry observers (and practitioners). But at the same time, it may have been our finest hour—a triumph of modern software engineering that averted a global catastrophe. Either way, the Y2K problem is likely to remain a footnote in the history of software engineering.

Software Engineering is a Social Activity

Software engineers work in teams, writing software components that are combined with the work of other software engineers in the construction of large systems. Teamwork is thus an essential ingredient in the process. Moreover, software engineers design systems to meet the requirements of end-users who are not software engineers, so having the social skills to interact with customers is also an important part of the development process.

Two significant problems with this reality are reflected in the film.

1. Software engineers as a whole—a point vociferously made by business analyst Tom Smykowski while explaining what it is he does at Initech—are not good with people.

2. These same people with the poor social skills, like the character Milton, are expected to function effectively on a team.

It is difficult not to sympathize with middle-aged Smykowski, the first to be downsized when Initech's business processes are re-engineered. During his interview with the efficiency consultants (the Bobs), Smykowski is asked "what would you say you do here?" Smykowski defensively explains that he takes the specs from the customers to the programmers, "because engineers are not good at dealing with customers." Smykowski typifies the raison d'etre of the modern day business analyst, whose sole job

73

qualification seems simply—as he bellows ironically—to "have people skills!" Smykowski's plight should serve as a reminder of the need to maintain technical relevancy: people skills alone are not enough.

Unlike Smykowski, the character Milton appears so completely socially retarded as to be unbelievable. To those of us in the industry, however, people like Milton are not an aberration. Indeed, some of the best programmers I've ever known share much of Milton's social awkwardness and obsessive-compulsive personality, which are likely symptomatic of Asperger's syndrome. As discussed in a previous essay, this mild form of autism is considered by some to be an advantage when it comes to the kind of thinking required to excel at software engineering.[1]

While Peter's patience is merely strained by Milton, other characters in the film openly mock Milton and his obsessive-compulsive disorder. In particular, Initech vice-president Bill Lumbergh delights in repeatedly asking Milton to move his desk simply because of the unease it causes him. Just like the archetypical alpha-male who steals the geek's ball and claims it was his in the first place, Lumbergh commandeers Milton's red Swingline stapler. Such open gestures of contempt for a team member as a means of exerting power and seeking popularity are unfortunate: management's bullying of the more socially challenged amongst our peers ultimately weakens the engineering team's performance.

Untested Programs Do Not Work

Peter's colleague Michael Bolton—the classic passive-aggressive nerd—feels both exploited and disrespected by his employer, despite his contributions to the firm's intellectual property (IP). Mi-

---

[1] Steve Silberman, "The geek syndrome," *Wired*, 9 (12), 2001.

chael's revenge is enacted when he unleashes a virus designed to slowly steal fractions of pennies during interest calculations on the credit union mainframe. However, the program is put into production without testing, and as Stroustrup succinctly puts it, "a program that has not been tested does not work."[2]

To Michael's dismay, his virus has a bug that causes way too much money to go missing, thus increasing the likelihood of its detection. He explains to his co-conspirators Peter and Samir that he must have had the decimal point in the wrong place, complaining that he always makes some stupid little mistake like that.

In truth, all software engineers make stupid little mistakes like that, all the time. In fact, it's often a complete shock to me that software works as well as it does given how:

• massively complex systems have become;

• escalated the corresponding attention to detail required to maintain these systems has become; and,

• easy it is to introduce run-time defects through simple typos and editing errors that escape compile-time detection.

This is why we test, and especially why we regression test after making even the most benign changes.

Not Everyone Gets to Write Video Games

Part of the apparent lack of job satisfaction indicated by the employees of Initech likely stems from the boring application area: banking software. We all want to work on the cool stuff, like

---

[2] Bjarne Stroustrup, *The C++ Programming Language (2rd ed.)* (Addison-Wesley, 1991), p. 380.

games, artificial intelligence, virtual reality, and porn websites. But let's face it, the majority of software engineering jobs are in mundane application areas like finance and corporate IT that involve straightforward information storage and retrieval.

Is Peter simply bored? Is Peter's career crisis caused by underutilization and a coincident lack of motivation? The Bobs certainly feel that Peter's problem is that he hasn't been challenged enough. They believe him when he explains "it's not that I'm lazy, it's that I just don't care." Software engineers should strive to find work environments and application areas that they find at least mildly interesting. If they don't, they risk Peter's predicament: if your only motivation is the fear of losing your job, you will only work just hard enough to avoid being fired. As discussed in a previous essay, software engineers should learn to assess where they are in the software engineer life cycle, and try to understand its effect on their productivity.

Brooks' Law

In his classic monograph on software engineering, *The Mythical-Man Month*, Fred Brooks describes the phenomenon whereby adding manpower to a late software project only serves to make it later. This counterintuitive result, which has become known as Brooks' Law, is largely due to the increased cost, time, and complexity of communication, training, coordination, and meetings when more manpower is involved.

A possible corollary to Brooks' Law is that within a software firm, individual programmer productivity is inversely correlated to company size. The larger the company, the less empowered programmers feel, or need to be; ineffectiveness can be hidden within the bureaucracy. I'll refer to this purely anecdotal observation as the Brooks Effect.

Initech is a case study in the Brooks Effect. While interviewing for his own job, Peter admits to the Bobs that "in a given week I probably only do about 15 minutes of real, actual work." The rest of his time is spent on such mundane activities as attending meetings, providing documentation, going for coffee with teammates, zoning out, filling out time-sheets (the infamous TPS Reports that serve as a running gag throughout the film), asking himself "is this good for the company?", playing Tetris, and eating birthday cake with coworkers.

A parody of the ubiquitous office birthday celebration is recreated with particular precision in *Office Space*. From the uninspired singing to the disingenuous show of appreciation, no detail is left unskewered. In reality, once a company reaches about 50 employees, there is a statistical likelihood of one birthday cake event per week. For some inexplicable reason, birthday celebrations often seem to be scheduled right before important activities that require intense concentration, like a code review. The stupor that invariably follows can only partly be blamed on hyperglycemia.

Case in point, in my one year of work for Bell-Northern Research, as one of over 4,000 employees, my entire output consisted of 16 mundane maintenance updates to the DMS-100 digital telephone switch software. During that time span, however, I did participate in over 30 birthday celebrations and three farewell luncheons (not including my own).

You Will Be Expected to Work Long Hours

Peter's boss Bill Lumbergh is a slightly exaggerated caricature of the prototypical alpha-male, and the film's most memorable character. Either a programmer who rode his social skills through the management track to the top of his game, or an exemplar of the

Dilbert Principle,[3] the always coffee-sipping and suspenders-wearing[4] Lumbergh seems primarily concerned that his employees accurately complete their weekly TPS Reports.

Lumbergh, who Peter believes represents "all that is soulless and wrong," doesn't hesitate to ask Peter to "go ahead and come in [Saturday]." The key phrase is *go ahead*, which suggests that Lum-

---

[3] *The Dilbert Principle* suggests that in many companies it is the worst employees who are promoted to management, because the company cannot afford to move the productive employees out of their current positions. Scott Adams, *The Dilbert Principle: A Cubicle's-Eye View of Bosses, Meetings, Management Fads, and Other Workplace Afflictions* (Harper Business, 1996).

[4] There is obviously a dress code at Initech (stated or implied) that forces all the men to wear a tie, even though they spend their day at a desk writing code. What on earth does wearing a tie have to do with programming? Why not specify that all software engineers have to wear a funny hat or wig? The tie is as necessary as a hat or wig, especially given (as Smykowski claimed) the software engineers are not allowed to meet with the customers. They made us wear a tie when I worked at IBM's software development lab in Toronto (and made us start work at 8:42 AM because of the unionized manufacturing plant next door), except for one dude who was such a compiler genius that he got away with wearing leather from head to toe. As an aside, you know your career is progressing nicely if you get to exert more control over your wardrobe with each new position or employer. But be warned: people will make assumptions about your socio-economic status based solely on how you are dressed. Theo, the doorman at my temporary apartment building in Cape Town, thought I was a bum who passed my time surfing while my girlfriend went to work every day. He had judged me based on the way that I dressed, and had no idea I had a doctorate and was CEO of a company. While the official uniform of software engineers is the unbuttoned dress shirt and khakis, I prefer sweat pants and a baggy t-shirt: comfortable, but apparently guaranteed chick repellant. "It's a good thing you are married, because you'll never get laid dressing like that" suggested my helpful queer eye at Smuggler's Cove Pub, where I spent too much of my time sitting at the bar, wearing sweat pants and riding the spiraling crashing waves of impotent despair as my marriage disintegrated. Of course, married or not, I wasn't getting laid. At least the bartender used to put on the alternative '80s station on the satellite whenever I was there. But I digress.

bergh thinks he is doing Peter a favor by letting him work over the weekend.

Software engineering—like many other professional positions such as law and medicine—is an occupation that can demand Herculean effort and extended work hours, particularly as deadlines approach. Overtime is rarely ever paid, despite efforts by jurisdictions such as California to legislate against the expectation of unpaid overtime. But the legality doesn't seem to matter, anyway, as many software engineers crave the intellectual calisthenics that programming offers, and will work overtime (or after-hours on open source projects) regardless of compensation. In this regard, Peter is an anomaly.

When Peter fails to show up to work on Saturday, Lumbergh launches a never-ending stream of telephone calls to Peter's home in an effort to locate and chastise his absent employee. This is my favorite scene in the film, not only for the comedic element of Lumbergh's distinctive greeting that begins each of his 17 recorded messages, but because it echoes my own personal experience with two different employers. While employees everywhere can relate to the inequity of the boss who parks the Porsche in the only reserved spot, it is these frantic voice messages, cell-phone calls, pages, instant messages, and urgent emails that are particularly endemic to the life of the software engineer on the mission critical path.

Is It All That Bad?

Towards the end of the film, Joanna counsels Peter that it is okay to be uninspired by his work, because "most people don't like their jobs." This is one moment where the film rings hollow, for in my experience, software engineers love their work. We may not like our boss, and the meetings, and the politics, but at the end of the day, there is nothing else we would rather be doing.

As I ease into my 40s, Peter's rhetorical question posed to Michael and Samir is particularly poignant: "what if we're still doing this when we're 50?" Personally, I sincerely hope I'm still doing this when I'm 50. As Lumbergh would say, *yeah, that would be great.*

End Notes

I am amazed at how accurate the depiction of the software development process and software engineers are in Douglas Coupland's *Microserfs* (Harper Collins, 1995) and his sort-of sequel *JPod* (Harper Collins, 2006).

The requirement to pay overtime to all software engineers was later overturned by California law S.B. 88 which exempts jobs that require skill and proficiency in the theoretical and practical application of highly specialized information to computer systems analysis, programming and software engineering.

An earlier version of this essay appeared in *Software Engineering Notes*, 30 (4), 2005.

A Seven-Layer Hierarchy of Careers in Computer Science

If your first job as a software engineer isn't all you had hoped for—good! Starting out at the bottom isn't necessary for you to learn the business; it's so you can learn some humility. You are no better than anyone else.

I once offered a job to a guy who described himself as a "creative generalist." We were looking for a project manager, but I offered him the position, anyway. Ultimately he refused the offer when I balked at his request for a MacBook Pro. I assumed the much cheaper Dell PC we already had could compute the critical path on a GANTT or PERT chart just as well as any Mac. He assumed I was an asshole for refusing his request.

In retrospect, my prima donna detector should have gone off when he described himself as both creative and a generalist. Don't get me wrong, creativity is an imperative skill if one wants to thrive in any software company, particularly one that builds games.[1] But a *generalist?* It's great to be good at many things, but

---

[1] Creativity is an often overlooked quality in good programmers. In 1956, IBM's first recruitment campaign for computer programmers was a print ad that targeted people who enjoyed algebra, music composition, and games, and who had lively imaginations. While not exactly the stereotype of today's computer nerd, it is a strikingly accurate set of criteria for the type of person who would be considered creative, logical, and likely enjoy programming. For more

being great at one thing is even gooder. Play to your strengths and specialize, kids. Nobody needs a generalist.

A Career Hierarchy

There are many different types of roles, titles, and employment positions in the information technology industries, and not all of them are created equally in terms of pay, prestige, desk size, and office location. These positions form a hierarchy; a ladder that an employee on their way to the top will climb over time (see Figure 8). Each successive rung comes with a new title, an increase in responsibility, and a coincident increase in remuneration.

The astute reader will detect three distinct paths through this directed acyclic graph that starts in the help desk and ends as a Chief Technology Officer (CTO) or other so-called C-level executive. Each path denotes a separate area of specialization. Programming moves through the middle of the diagram. Quality assurance (QA) and quality control (QC) moves along the left, while systems administration along the right. In other words, you can specialize in writing the software, or in ensuring its quality, or in optimizing the environment on which it runs.

One thing that might surprise the reader—particularly the undergraduate—is that the programmer is in the *middle* of the hierarchy, not at the bottom. From humble beginnings you shall build your empire. The humblest positions provide customer service tech support to the end users. You won't necessarily start your post-graduation career in support, but don't be surprised if (like me) you end up there on your first co-op work term placement.

---

on this fascinating story, see Nathan Ensmenger, "Building Castles in the Air: Reflections on recruiting and training programmers during the early period of computing," *Communications of the ACM*, 54 (4), pp. 28-30.

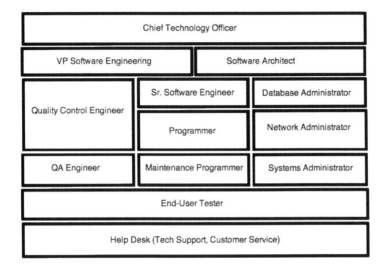

Figure 8. A typical career hierarchy for computer scientists working in a large software engineering enterprise. I have deliberately excluded other soft-skilled specialties such as the business analyst and project manager as those jobs are typically filled by non-computer science grads.

Sometimes the stint in support is temporary. The founders of AbeBooks.com made it a policy that all new hires (programmers included) started their employment with at least two weeks as part of the customer service team. Answering email and troubleshooting problems reported by the customers (used booksellers) was seen as a good way for new hires to learn the business. It also created a sense of team that pervaded the enterprise.

Customer service is a great skill, and a good place to practice problem solving. Being good at it is all about empathy for the person having the problem with your product or service. If you worked in food service or retail when you were younger, you would have had plenty of practice. Don't be fooled: helping others is hard work. It is sometimes boring, and with the wrong attitude it can become exhausting. Those with the energy to provide support with a smile and a sense of humour, day in and day out, are very special. Almost as special as the people who think it is okay to humiliate and abuse them.[2]

Software Testing as a Specialty

Quality software is a software product that meets the requirements as defined by the documents produced during the requirements phase of its life cycle. Most software engineering textbooks define **quality assurance** as the activity of defining the standards used in the software process, whereas **quality control** is the activity of overseeing the process to ensure that standards are followed. However, the software industry tends to hand out the title *quality assurance engineer* to anyone involved in testing software, not just those higher ups that make methodology decisions. The difference between defining standards and following standards is often blurred. This is particularly the case in small, immature organizations (in the Capability Maturity Model sense of maturity[3]) that have yet to codify a set of quality assurance standards.

Without any proactive attempt to improve programming productivity through the introduction, enforcement, and measurement of programming standards and configuration management, there is no need to distinguish one tester from another in the quality assurance team. The hierarchy in Figure 8 attempts to capture the

---

[2] If you are in a relationship with someone who is regularly abusive and dismissive with wait staff and telephone support personnel, don't be surprised when he/she ends up treating you just as poorly.

[3] The Capability Maturity Model was developed by Carnegie Mellon University as a way to assess and improve an organization's software development process. See *The Capability Maturity Model: Guidelines for Improving the Software Process* (Addison-Wesley Professional, 1994).

trajectory of testing roles within more mature software development shops by distinguishing between assurance and control engineering.

End-user testers are those members of the testing team that treat the software product as an opaque black-box. They do not look at the source code. Anyone capable of using and understanding the software product is more or less up to the task being an end-user tester. End-user testers are responsible for the creation of **test cases,** which detail the procedure for testing a specific program function. The test case is a document that lists a sequence of inputs and their expected output. The testers then "run" these test cases in order to reveal the presence of bugs. The tester's responsibility is to exercise the software and discover as many bugs as possible as quickly as possible. The reliability of a program is increased as errors are discovered and removed. The end-user tester believes the testing phase of the life cycle is over when all the test cases can be run without revealing any errors.

A *QA engineer* is the title I reserve specifically for white-box testers. These testers are allowed to look at the source code, and they improve quality through static analysis (code reviews) and/or the creation of test cases designed to exercise as many paths through the code as possible. While it is possible to employ someone with no programming expertise as an end-user tester, the QA engineer's job requires programming skill and the reasoning ability to perform coverage-based testing. The adoption of unit testing as a coding discipline, and its automated support through excellent tools like JUnit, has shifted much of the white-box testing burden to programmers. But I suspect that for the foreseeable future QA engineers will continue to enforce coding standards through program inspections and will also ensure that programmers create unit tests that meet a prescribed level of path coverage.

The *QC engineer* defines coding standards, decides which integrated development environment will be used, creates documentation templates, and provides other anal-retentive checklists associated with engineering rigor. The buck stops here: the QC engineer decides when the product is ready to ship. Not all organizations or projects are large enough to afford the luxury of a QC engineer, but when they do have one, that person is usually also in charge of the code repository, the scripts used to build release candidates, software configuration management, version control, and possibly the staging environment where release candidates are exercised by the end-user testers.

The QC engineer is the software police of the organization. The QC engineer is the person who publicly shames you by kicking your ass around the office for an hour when your latest check-in breaks the build and brings the testing effort to a grinding halt.

Tester versus Programmer: the Eternal Struggle

Amidst all that creative energy poured into building software, testing remains the one destructive activity. Perhaps because of this creative-destructive dichotomy, the prevailing view in the culture of our industry is that testers are somehow less skilled than developers. This misconception often causes testing to become a ghetto of lower paid, less educated individuals with low self-esteem. Because they are often deprived of opportunities for advancement, testers justifiably feel an unhealthy resentment for the programmers and managers, whom they perceive as the Man who is keeping them down.

Testing is monumentally important and requires a high skill level in order to do the task effectively. This begs the question, why do we put morons in the test department? Moreover, why shouldn't we put computer scientists in test? In my experience, computer scientists don't make very good software testers. As a computer science student, I learned how to create software systems. I equated my chosen profession with the creative process of problem solving through programming. Giving me a testing role is asking me to do something completely opposite to what I was taught. Because unsatisfactory results are highly probable, I'm just not the right person for the job. But then who is?

How about if we make testers out of the kids who laughed at you and bullied you when you were growing up? This might be a good idea for two reasons: they would probably be good at it; and you, the programmer, would enjoy the smug satisfaction of knowing you make more money than they do. Kind of like the irony of Biff waxing George McFly's car at the end of *Back to the Future*.

Programmer	Tester
Creative	Critical
Played with Lego	Tried to light Lego on fire
Excitable	Calm
Under strict deadlines	Doesn't give a shit about deadlines
Trained to write programs	Trained to find fault with others
Wears glasses	Enjoys breaking glass
Ralph and Piggy	Jack and Roger
Brian Johnson	John Bender

Table 1. The Tester is the foil of the Programmer.

The programmer and tester share the same goal of delivering robust software in a timely manner, but the means they employ are different: the programmer tries to make it work, while the tester tries to make it fail. They must avoid feelings of animosity if their working environment is to remain healthy. This is particularly true of the programmer, who should take care to avoid regarding the tester as the enemy. Because the programmer is likely under pressure to produce "correct" code before a set deadline, the tension between tester and programmer is understandable—the tester threatens the deadlines that the programmer seeks to meet. While the tension between tester and programmer (see Table 1) is natural, it is exacerbated by programmers who feel their self-worth is defined by their work (a so-called human *doing* rather than a human being); an attack on their code is tantamount to a personal attack.

If you are testing someone's code, be sensitive to the possibility that that they will see you as a threat.

If you are an overly sensitive programmer, try to separate your work from your self worth. It is irrational to think of the tester as an enemy—your tester is a teammate who covers home plate for you in case you let that throw from the outfield accidentally get by you.

Flavours of Programmers

The career path for programmers (Figure 8) has several stages and usually begins with the job of *maintenance programmer* (also known as a *junior software engineer*). When an employee is new, a great way to learn a complex software system is to try and maintain it. Fixing bugs and adding incremental features exposes you to the design ideas of other programmers, and perhaps more importantly, it will educate you about the common causes of mistakes.

As maintenance programmers become more confident, they may even try their hands at **refactoring**: fixing something that ain't broke for the purpose of making it more efficient, readable, or easy to maintain gives the rookie engineer the chance to redesign some of the overgrown code.

When a maintenance programmer graduates from working on someone else's old program to getting to work on new products, they are promoted to *programmer*, or sometimes the loftier title of *software engineer*. Congratulations—you are now finally allowed to do what you did in school for years.

The person leading a team of programmers is the s*enior software engineer*. Team leaders supervise the work of others, and after conducting regularly scheduled performance reviews they make recommendations to management regarding promotions and pay raises. The senior software engineer is also responsible for the bulk of the ad-hoc design work and refactoring that is often necessary to augment the omissions and errors that were committed by the software architect during the design phase of the life cycle.

Speaking of which, the *software architect*—also known as a *software designer*, and historically as a *systems analyst*—is in charge of the design phase of the life cycle and the documentation of the software architecture. The software architect is a seasoned programmer who instinctively knows effective ways to decompose systems into processes, threads, classes, libraries—whatever it takes. This person typically produces an object-oriented decomposition that employs patterns like Model-View-Controller[4] when they are appropriate. The software architect employs object-oriented de-

---

[4] The Model-View-Controller (MVC) pattern isolates two design decisions regarding an entity: the underlying data structure and its operations (the model) and how it is presented to the user (the view). The controller glues them together in the code that processes input events from the view and applies them to the model. An entity, by the way, is a real or abstract thing about which we store data.

composition patterns, not because they have read the patterns book, but because they have been using them appropriately since long before someone bothered to name them.

The software architect is also an accomplished data modeler, capable of producing an entity-relationship diagram that is normalized appropriately and easily converted to an elegant underlying relational database schema. If you want to be an architect, be sure to learn your SQL and relational database theory.

Flavours of Programming

As an academic discipline, computer science traditionally differentiates between three core research areas: *systems*, *applications*, and *theory*. Often the curriculum includes a requirement that undergraduates take a certain number of courses within each area. While it is becoming more common to see software engineering as a fourth area, or a separate department altogether, historically it was considered part of the applications area.

Coincident with this taxonomy, the workplace has long distinguished between two categories of software engineers: *systems programmers*, and *application programmers*.

Systems programmers are software engineers who write software tools and libraries like operating systems, device drivers, web servers, and network programming stacks. Systems programmers write programs for other software engineers to use through an application programmer interface (API). In other words, systems programmers work on the software we study in computer science courses that fall into the systems area, such as operating systems, network programming, and real-time systems.

Conversely, application programmers are software engineers who use APIs and their software libraries to build applications for end-users who are laypersons. Shrink-wrap consumer software, office productivity suites, games, web applications, and enterprise software are all built by application programmers for a particular market of consumers or for a specific client.

A recent trend differentiates between application programmers who use traditional operating system APIs to create standalone programs for dedicated platforms like Windows, and those who build web applications for the platform agnostic web browser. This distinction is necessary because there are fundamental differences between the two. Web application programmers require working knowledge of the HTTP protocol, SQL, and at least one of the competing frameworks for making it all possible given the underlying stateless nature of HTTP.

So if you want to focus on programming as your specialty, first decide between systems and applications. And if you want to build applications, decide between web-based and stand-alone.

Entitlement Makes You Look Pretty Ugly

Thom Yorke—influential voice of a generation as the lead singer of Radiohead—had it wrong. It's not ambition that makes you look pretty ugly; it's your sense of entitlement. There is nothing wrong with being ambitious. But you can't expect to take any shortcuts on your journey to the top. Provided there is a clear path to advancement to the next layer, entering the career hierarchy near the bottom is a good idea: regardless of the pursuit, paying your dues makes you a more humble, compassionate person.

Shed your entitlement, or risk being labeled a prima donna and shown the door. Software engineering is a team effort, and nobody wants a teammate who only makes an effort to work on what he wants to do instead of what needs to be done. If you find yourself in the test department, accept the challenge and give it your all. Test is a ghetto only if you stubbornly refuse to pick up a copy of Myers' *The Art of Software Testing*, immerse yourself in the mathematics of equivalence classes and boundary cases, and grasp the mantle.

Before I was given the opportunity to join a project team as a programmer and craft my first piece of virgin 1.0 code, I paid my dues in tech support, testing, and maintenance. Working for very large private corporations like IBM and Bell-Northern Research, both with long histories of building and maintaining large software systems, exposed me to the engineering rigor necessary to manage software projects involving hundreds of team members. I recommend that new graduates spend at least a year or two working for a similarly sized organization and pay attention to how they manage complexity.

While I am now able to view my early career experience as valuable, I have to admit that at the time I was often angry and frustrated—*this isn't why I went to university*, I would think to myself. You may not need to fill these roles in order to learn the ropes, but it is a good idea to learn how difficult it is to do these jobs for an extended period of time without going nuts. As a result, I believe that I have learned to treat people with respect, no matter what their role in the organization.

At the end of my programming career I was a senior software engineer at Prophet.Net in Palo Alto, California. Originally hired in August of 2000 as a consulting web application developer, I was soon asked if I knew anything about systems programming. Tim Knight—founder of Prophet.Net—promised me a life-time of employment if I could somehow create a real-time stock market ticker plant server to replace the expensive and unreliable one they were licensing. Completed in just under one year, *Market-Maker* (as it was dubbed) became a cornerstone of the website's back end, and a key piece of IP for Prophet.Net. Clocking in at just over 30,000 lines of C/C++ for Windows 2000 (yes, Windows—Linux sucks), MarketMaker enabled Tim to provide innovative and unique intraday trading tools for his customers. True to his word, Tim kept me on retainer, and I earned a comfortable living fixing bugs, adding new features, and porting MarketMaker to 64-bit Windows.

In 2005, Tim sold Prophet.Net to Investools for $9M. Due to the importance of MarketMaker as a proprietary piece of IP, I felt my personal contribution to the $9M valuation of Prophet.Net was significant. At that moment I promised myself that the next time I wrote a million dollar piece of software, it would be for me.[5]

More importantly, the acquisition of Prophet.Net opened a door for me to expand my consulting business and hire my first employees. That summer I quit teaching software engineering and got down to business.

End Notes

The title of this essay is a reference to the OSI Seven Layer Model of data communication, an idealized abstraction of how a hierarchy of software modules can be used to deal with the complexity of building a reliable computer network.

I was busy pouting and generally being an ass during my work-term as an end-user tester on the System/38 team at IBM—until I started reading *The Art of Software Testing* (John Wiley & Sons, 1979) by Glenford J. Myers. The opening chapter will change

---

[5] It turns out that Chris Hoefgen wrote my million dollar piece of software, but at least *Scratch and Win* for Facebook was my idea. That is probably how it is supposed to work. Hang in there, Chris. Your turn is next.

your perspective in a hurry, and maybe even genuinely turn you on to the intellectual challenge of being an effective software tester.

I could never understand why everyone got such a boner for the "patterns book," but if you are new to design it is always good to look at how the experts approach some recurring problems in software engineering. *Design Patterns: Elements of Reusable Object-Oriented Software* (Addison-Wesley, 1994) is by the so-called Gang of Four: Erich Gamma, Richard Helm, Ralph Johnson, and John M. Vlissides. Also by Gang of Four is the highly-recommended 1982 studio album *Songs of the Free*.

Radiohead's song *Paranoid Android* off their 1997 album *OK Computer* includes the lyric "ambition makes you look pretty ugly." Any album entitled *OK Computer* is recommended listening for software engineers, regardless of whether you are testing, coding, or administering. You've gotta love a profession where listening to music all day long doesn't interfere with your ability to work. By the way, why is it possible to listen to music and program at the same time? I think of programming as visualizing a temporal simulation of the changes to an abstract structure according to the instructions contained in a poem; how is it that listening to a song doesn't interfere with that process? Is there a correlation between musical ability and programming acumen? If so, does it have something to do with the close similarity between a musical score and a program (both of which describe a sequence of events using a highly compact notation)?

What's Your Secret Sauce?

I woke up one day to discover I was CEO of a social gaming company.

Before the success of our games on Facebook, Backstage was a contract software engineering firm that built stock market trading tools for investors.[1] We were not a computer game company in any sense of the word, but we did know how to do two important things very well: build scalable web applications, and keep customers happy. In hindsight, exactly the kind of DNA required to be a great social gaming company.

When we first launched *Scratch and Win* on Facebook in September of 2007 (the very early days of third-party apps), we didn't even think of it as a game. In our minds, it was a gifting app that had a virtual gambling component. Over time, as we added stages, achievements, limited-edition collections of prize sets, and a marketplace for in-game trading between players, we realized that the virtual economy was a game, where players competed to maximize their social status. *The economy is the game*™ is a paradigm we like to think we invented (or at least trademarked).

Like most internet start-ups, I founded Backstage Technologies with the intention to sell it for millions of dollars. Our mission statement was to do something cool and be acquired by Google

---

[1] And before that, Backstage wrote control software for audio networks. Third time really is a charm.

for $20M. Conversely, our core value was that the absence of pants greatly reduces ass sweat.

The first time we were in negotiations to be acquired was the summer of 2009. Talks lasted about three days, but during that time, the VP of business development from the prospective acquirer kept warning us not to divulge any of the ingredients in our "secret sauce," lest the deal fall apart (which it did) and we ended up suing them for stealing all our invaluable IP (which hasn't happened... yet).

Every time he used the phrase *secret sauce*, which was often, I found myself becoming more and more amused. What the heck is a secret sauce? I assumed he meant competitive edge, or IP, but being a marketing type, he liked using that buzzword instead. Wikipedia tells me that secret sauce means any component of a product that is closely guarded from public disclosure for competitive advantage.

So, what exactly was Backstage's secret sauce? Did we even have one? We certainly did, and the primary ingredient was the knowledge of how to design and build a social game, and its underlying virtual economy, that was both engaging and monetized well. That certainly constituted a fair portion of our secret sauce.

But our *special* sauce was not a secret to any of our competitors—it was our commitment to customer service. Anyone can steal that, but it takes a huge commitment.

Like it or not, software engineers are in the service industry. Recall from an earlier chapter that software engineers construct software tools for humanity. Any piece of software you create will have a customer, end-user, client (programmer or program), or stake-holder. The *software-as-a-service* paradigm makes this clear.

From a business perspective, how you manage the customer relationship is important to the successful adoption of your product. The guiding principles of customer service that we adopted at Backstage were as follows.

1. **Have an open and honest dialogue with your customers.** Admit when you have made a mistake, apologize, and make amends through some form of compensation.

2. **Show empathy.** If a customer has a complaint or problem and is asking you to fix it, don't take it personally or get defensive. While I won't go so far as to say that customer complaints are a gift, at least the customers care enough to take the time to reach out. The least you can do is acknowledge that you have heard them. Starting a response with "I hear you and understand where you are coming from" does wonders to begin a fruitful exchange. So does asking for more information to ensure you fully understand the issue. Sometimes the customer just wants to be heard, and to know that a real person is listening.

3. **Never argue or debate with a customer.** You will never win an argument with a customer, particularly in a public forum. Instead, provide information, or as Sergeant Joe Friday would say, "just the facts, ma'am." Editorializing, sarcasm, and name-calling are not the hallmarks of good customer service, but self-deprecating humour can be a useful tool to defuse an irate customer. Kill them with kindness.

4. The customer isn't always right, but the **paying customers tend to be more right than others.**

To summarize, the role of the public-facing customer service representative is to provide information in an honest and empathetic manner and to prioritize responses by putting the paying customers first.

Conversely, the role of a chief executive officer (CEO) of a startup company is to do four things.

1. Define company culture.

2. Hire the management team.

3. Raise capital to fund expansion.

4. Set high-level goals, and implement strategies to achieve these goals.

When we first launched *Scratch and Win*, I handled all of the customer service. I felt the job was too important to be trusted to anyone else in the organization. Unlike a lot of CEOs who pay lip service to how important customer service is, I put my money where my mouth was and actually put in the hours to respond to posts on the discussion boards and answer every single email from our growing customer base. Given the viral nature of social networks, I figured the investment in building a loyal fan-base and branding Backstage as a company that cared about its user community would ultimately pay off. I also hoped that my leadership-by-example would result in a customer-centric culture at Backstage.

I remained in charge of customer service until it reached a point (almost a year later) where I could no longer devote the time and attention required to do the job justice. I still made the occasional appearance on the discussion boards, but my community managers were happy to relegate me to pseudo-mythical status (see Figure 9).

Our competitors built their business on monetization. We built ours on customer service. Here is a typical post to the discussion board for *Scratch and Win* that illustrates the point.

Efrain Rivera Junior wrote 5 hours ago

I've been playing Facebook applications for a while now. I usually participate in all the games forums at one point or another. And I have to say that the ONLY application in which I ALWAYS receive an answer from a game developer has been in S&W. Not only that, but most of my ideas have been implemented in the game, and the rest have at least been listened to. Not only have I NEVER received an answer from any other application dev, but also I was once banned from a game for making a simple suggestion (needless to say, that app is no longer on Facebook). Therefore, I want to thank the devs of Scratch & Win for being so active and nice. As always, thanks for listening.

No, Efrain—thank you for playing.

Figure 9. *Russ versus the Squid,* part of a *Scratch and Win* stage 8 prize set. Is it just me or do I look slightly light on my loafers? I blame Myke Allen, the artist.

Having defined our corporate culture, "we care for our customers more than the competition," I focused my efforts on the next three roles of the CEO. If any of you reading this little monograph have the ambition to one day lead a startup hi-tech company, be sure you are capable of making the important transition from CTO to VP of Sales (or understand when you need to hire a VP of Sales as part of the management team). Ultimately, the failure of many startup CEOs is their inability to recognize the tipping point when the company will either fly, or crash on the tarmac. Our tipping point came in the autumn of 2009, when Zynga introduced *FarmVille* and changed the landscape of social gaming.

Doing a Deep-Dive into our Secret Sauce in order to Move the Needle

Like many small Facebook game developers, we hit some turbulence in the autumn of 2009. That turbulence was named *FarmVille*, and the beast wouldn't sleep until it had sucked up all of our user's microtransactions like a giant Hoover in search of buried coins in the sofa. Not only did Zynga's mega-hit dominate attention cycles, it raised the bar regarding user expectations of what a game on Facebook was all about. Suddenly our new players—those we could manage to acquire as our apps fought for attention on a News Feed dominated by stories about virtual farming—weren't monetizing like they used to. Our long-time players were still spending, but at a diminished rate. What to do?

Secretly Canadian, we felt disadvantaged by our location, which made it difficult to access Facebook or tap into the network of venture capitalists clustered around the Silicon Valley. Earlier in the decade I had worked for five years at Prophet.Net in Palo Alto, witnessing firsthand the tons of superbly ordinary people who ride the coattails of a few Valley visionaries. I knew my team was world class and that what we had accomplished was extraordinary. But I also knew we could very easily become the VisiCalc of social gaming, destined to be a long forgotten footnote in a history to be written by those who came after.

Undeterred, we rolled up our sleeves and started to gather information. A quick survey of our user community suggested that many of our higher-stage players had noticed that our virtual currency wasn't a good deal anymore. Our games award players a limited amount of free daily Credits to spend, and we made money by selling more to those who were impatient about waiting until the next day. However, as players advanced through our games, their free daily Credit allotment increased, and so reduced the inherent value of the currency of those who spent to acquire more. Our attempts to mitigate Credit devaluation by offering bulk discounts to higher stage players had collapsed. Had Backstage jumped the shark?

Not so fast, bucko. After an honest exchange with the team at SuperRewards, and a focus group made up of a cross-section of our core audience, we decided to invest in optimizing our virtual currency so that the stage could be set for our upcoming development efforts. The solution was going to be important and painful. Important, because it meant that we could open up additional avenues to monetization and turn new users into monetizing users sooner than before. Painful because it required a significant software change that would delay new product development.

By the end of 2009, we had an effective and scalable solution in place in the form of a new, premium currency on all of our apps: Backstage Bucks (B$). Users would now buy/earn B$, instead of free in-game Credits, and all of our virtual goods were priced in both Credits and B$.

However, managing a change of this magnitude wasn't as quick or easy as we had hoped. A minor protest erupted in our user community as a result of B$, which made it clear to our long-term users (some of whom had been loyal Backstage players for two years) that there was a competitive  advantage to those who spent real money in our apps. Fortunately, the pain was short-lived. We weathered the storm of user confusion and learned how to optimize pricing and content releases so that our players who didn't pay felt respected and fairly treated, while our paying players still experienced some advantage.

Optimizing our existing revenue streams was only going to marginally move the needle. Ultimately, we needed to build our own Zynga-like mega-hit. *FarmVille* had opened our eyes to the real possibility of the medium, and what social gaming 2.0 would be.

In fulfilling the third role of the CEO, I secured a private round of investment. The capital helped to solidify our development team and enabled us to get to work on some new apps. Never shy of ideas, Backstage had accumulated a pipeline of game designs that we were itching to launch. *Family Feud* (see Figure 10)—a joint venture with casual gaming company iWin—was waiting in the wings, and would ultimately become our greatest hit yet.

My Board of Directors—whose capacity for Backstage bullishness seemed unbridled and boundless—told me that a turnaround in the face of adversity would feel more satisfying than the joy we had felt from our initial success. Once we did the necessary deep-dive into understanding what had happened, and had figured out how to correct it, the ensuing high-fives would create a deafening cacophony that emanated from the third floor of our Chinatown studio.

Figure 10. The author shows off an early version of *Family Feud,* **developed jointly by Backstage and iWin.** Our partner iWin had the awesome Flash version of the game that we embedded within our social game framework. It was our idea to limit the number of free daily episodes (which drove monetization), and to require that you invite a friend to complete the back half of the fast money round (which drove virality). Greg Patrick was the Backstage lead programmer on this project. *Family Feud* is a trademark of FreemantleMedia, who licensed the property to iWin. Success has many fathers, whereas failure is an orphan. Photo by Myke Allen.

Exactamundo. High-fives, everybody.

I am so proud of what we accomplished, and I owe a huge debt of gratitude to our customers, my team, and our business partners and colleagues in the social gaming industry. But we made some mistakes. If I had to do it all over again I would be less risk-averse and a lot more aggressive. My lack of self-esteem made me unwilling to accept our success as wholly deserved, and this worked against us. We might have been as big as Zynga, but we acted too cautiously. We should have taken a slightly lower road, and borrowed a page or two from their playbook by cloning other people's great ideas and cross-promoting to our existing user base.

On September 13, 2010, three years to the day that *Scratch and Win* debuted on Facebook, Backstage became a wholly-owned subsidiary of RealNetworks. Under new ownership, the days of Backstage being the apologetic, trepidatious little Canadian studio are long gone. Now, they can build the billion dollar social game.

End Notes

VisiCalc was the first spreadsheet application for personal computers. It lost market share to Lotus 1-2-3, which eventually lost to Microsoft Excel.

SuperRewards (now part of AdKnowledge) was an early virtual currency monetization service for Facebook application developers. I met Jason Bailey, founder of SuperRewards, at the inaugural Vancouver Facebook Developer Garage in November of 2007. Two months later, *Scratch and Win* became the first application to integrate SuperRewards.

Our *Family Feud* partnership arose from a meeting with David Fox, then iWin VP of Technology, at Casual Connect 2009 in Seattle.

The Backstage Board of Directors consisted of Alex Rampell (Co-Founder/CEO of TrialPay), Rasool Rayani (Co-Founder of MetaLogix), Daryl Hatton (Founder/CEO of ConnectionPoint Systems), me, and David Ovans (father of the CEO). Nepotism makes the world go 'round.

At the time of acquisition, the management team at Backstage was Marc Dugas, Chris Hoefgen, Dave Kelsey, Greg Patrick, and Alex Mendelev. You guys rock.

Pandemonium Reigned

This book is my midlife crisis.

I got divorced at the age of 40. Leaving a bad marriage enabled me to enjoy a crisis of identity that led to the success of Backstage, which in turn prompted me to write this book.

But why write this book now, at this age and stage of my life? I used to be able to write to entertain, but then I went to grad school and learned to write in a formal, academic style. I wondered if I had permanently dulled those neural pathways that were involved in writing goofy short stories when I was younger, especially the one that ended up giving the kids in my high school something else to make fun of other than my intense social awkwardness, lankiness, glasses, and braces?

I wrote a story once that included the sentence "Pandemonium reigned." It was actually a line that I had stolen from a guy named Gordon who had penned it during a typing class on Salt Spring Island. It was the year that through some quirk of scheduling, the grade 10 boys at Gulf Islands Secondary School all had to take either typing or cooking as one of their electives. I wanted to take woodworking, but settled for typing as the lesser of the two feminine evils offered to us. It was during one of our early typing classes that Gordon started to write some entertaining short stories that involved ordinary people suddenly finding themselves in outrageous situations or performing irresponsible acts of mayhem. And indeed one of his stories included the hilarious (to me at least) sentence "Pandemonium reigned" when describing one of these situations. If I recall correctly, this particular masterpiece involved a young man driving angrily at high speed in a stolen car and randomly blowing up people and things, in a somewhat prescient take on Michael Douglas's character in the film *Falling Down*.

With minimal adult supervision, we acted like boys marooned in a typing classroom. Bored with the study of business letter formats and the proper construction of typed footnotes, we started to follow Gordon's lead. I began to look forward to typing class because it had deteriorated into a kind of drum circle of timed-speed contests and story-writing bravado. While I soon eclipsed Gordon's skills as a typist, nobody could touch his mastery of amusing and bizarre fiction.

When my family relocated to suburban Victoria that spring, two newfound things came with me: a penchant for typing, and a surreal story-writing sensibility. When I was asked to choose my courses for the latter half of the year at my new high school, I had no choice but to add typing (since I was only halfway through what I had started on Salt Spring), but also chose creative writing (since I was always pretty good at writing). In hindsight, I don't know why it hadn't occurred to me that I would be the only boy enrolled in typing. I was also the only student enrolled in creative writing who was actually thrilled to get credit for making up stories. While I could manage to hide during my afternoon typing class, my love for creative writing was soon outed by Mrs. Taylor's habit of posting the stories she found most entertaining at the back of the classroom. One of these stories was my own take on one of Gordon's extravaganzas, replete with that killer sentence, *Pandemonium reigned.*

Whether karma, cosmic justice, or coincidence, this simple act of plagiarism would lead to my suffering the ridicule and scorn of my peers.

A boy named Dale was one of my fellow creative writing students, and he apparently did not share my love for Gordon's writing style. Unfortunately, Dale wasn't content simply to tell the others about the weird and nerdy stories written by the new guy; he felt it was necessary to show them firsthand. After he stole my story from the back wall of the classroom, he proceeded to spread it like a virus through literally every person in our grade. I think he might have even made photocopies. Unsure what to make of me and my writing, the kids at school somehow decided that the best way to deal with me was to make fun of my work. I thus became known as Pandemonium Reigned.

For the remainder of that school year, when I wasn't being alienated and ignored, kids would yell across the rows of lockers at me, "Hey, Panda-moniummmmmmm!" I'm not sure how many of my abusers actually knew what the word meant, or how many of them imagined that it was raining pandemonium. I did know, however, that this nickname was not helping me make friends.

So it was with some poetic irony that Dale and I would grow to become close friends, and eventually carpooled for a time during our university years. But it wasn't until 12 years after his act of thievery that he admitted his responsibility in the crime. While standing at the urinals during our ten year high school reunion, Dale broke the cardinal rule of male etiquette and spoke to me, explaining that the whole "pandemonium thing" was an act of "intellectual jealousy." What I couldn't explain in return, for at that point I could hardly admit to an act of intellectual theft, was that it didn't hurt so much as confuse. How could something as unimportant as a short-story be so misunderstood and misconstrued at my new school, yet so loved and lauded in a typing class of boys a short ferry ride away?

I guess the medium really is the message.

Epilogue: Redemption through Introspection

Address your inner injuries before a lack of self-esteem destroys your prospects for career advancement.

If you skipped the *Preface*, now would be a good time to read it.

Sometimes I fear that my ex-wife wants me to continue to be sad, lonely, and give her all my money. In other words, she wishes we were still married.

When a marriage begins to fail, and you no longer feel safe in sharing your true self or feelings with your partner, it can seem like the loneliest place on earth. If you were single, you could reach out to others in an appropriate manner, but when you are married, you are constrained. The result is a train wreck of secrecy, and a search elsewhere for the fulfillment and validation that you no longer experience with your spouse. Not surprisingly, pornography, cybersex, gambling, drugs, alcohol and other forms of self-medication become increasingly attractive. When you are single, you can simply join a running club.

That I managed to keep my professional career on track during the eight years of staying married "for the sake of the children" is somewhat miraculous. At least that's what I thought, until years after our split when it became apparent that my career had actually been suffering—like the proverbial frog in the boiling water, I simply hadn't noticed. It is impossible to separate the quality of your work from the quality of your life. If you can help it, don't repeat my mistakes.

Since software engineering is a social activity, it behooves us to address our inner injuries before a lack of self-esteem destroys our careers. Don't blame others. It is rarely (if ever) someone else's fault when things go wrong for you at work. Through introspection, learn about your weaknesses and your inadequacies. Embrace them. Love yourself despite them, and then strive to overcome them. Seek help in this process, for objectivity is a difficult skill to master at first. But the rewards are worth it. In acquiring empathy and thoughtfulness, you will learn to play nice with your colleagues. They, in turn, will play nice with you.

Try to remember this: we're all just doing the best we can.

Now get out there and bust some heads.

Feedback: rovans@acm.org

Join the Facebook discussion: http://facebook.com/LOTFiles

The author wishes to acknowledge the suggestions and encouragement of Rob Lockstone, Meghan McDermott, Devin Stenson, Will Tracz, and Grenfell Featherstone, and to thank his parents for making him what he is.

Made in the USA
San Bernardino, CA
09 January 2014